DEAR TEACHERS:

We, the editors of *Creative Classroom*, frequently hear from teachers about how much they enjoy using the A+ Activities and seasonal Kids' Pages in our magazine. Now, for the first time, we have combined them both in this handy paperback volume—*Creative Classroom A+ Activities.*

We selected some of the best ideas from our teacher-created A+ Activities column and divided them by curriculum areas. Then we added extension ideas, useful resources, strategies for adapting the activities for older or younger students, cross-curricular suggestions, and a list of the national standards they meet. Whether these A+ Activities are used by themselves, or in combination with our seasonal pages, you have a wealth of ready-made lessons at your fingertips.

Keep our book close at hand for immediate ways to add variety to your everyday K-6 curriculum and to enhance your lessons. We guarantee that *Creative Classroom A+ Activities* will save you time and money—and keep your teaching fresh!

Susan K. Evento

Susan K. Evento
Editorial Director

Creative Director **CHRISTINE BACZEWSKA**

Editorial Director **SUSAN K. EVENTO**

Associate Editor **LAURA PYE**

Assistant Editor **MELISSA E. NORKIN**

Copy Editor **MARGARET MITTELBACH**

Proofreader **MICHAEL CREWDSON**

Creative Classroom A+ Activities

ISBN: 0-9711879-0-8

Published in 2001 by Creative Classroom Publishing, LLC, 149 Fifth Avenue, 12th floor, New York, NY 10010.

Printed in the United States of America.

10 9 8 7 6 5 4 3 2 1

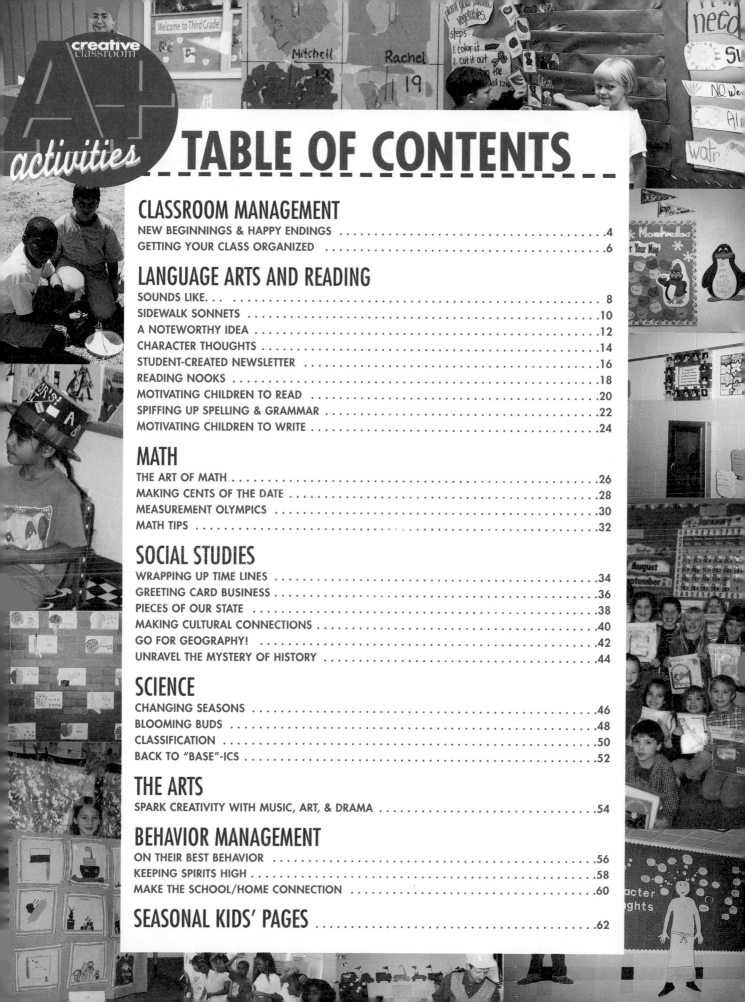

TABLE OF CONTENTS

NEW BEGINNINGS

The *ABC*'s of Success

After the long summer break, students always need to be reminded of study skills and appropriate school behavior. Rather than lecturing them, I assign a letter of the alphabet to each student. They then think of study skills or school rules that begin with their letters. For example, students may think of "**G**et to class on time" or "**B**ring a pencil every day." Next, they write the phrases and draw accompanying pictures on heavy-stock paper. We then share the phrases and hang them above the chalkboard in alphabetical order to serve as reminders throughout the school year.

—*Kay Krause*
Berwyn, PA

Getting to Know You

I begin the school year with an activity that shows kids how much they have in common with each other. On separate pieces of paper, I write statements such as, "I have a dog" or "I like to play ping pong." I give one statement to each child. Then students walk around our room and ask classmates whether they agree with the statement. If they do, they sign the piece of paper. After collecting the papers, we tabulate responses and make an "Our Class Interests" bar graph. Finally, we post the signed papers around the graph. This activity helps spark some great friendships among students.

—*LuAnn Smith*
Denver, CO

NEW FACES

During the first week of school, students use "multicultural construction paper" and other art materials to create self-portraits. We attach them to a bulletin board outside our classroom that displays our class motto. As students pass the bulletin board on their way to class, it helps set the tone for the day—and the year ahead.

—*Lori Christopoulos and Angie Castleberry*
Tulsa, OK

OUR CELEBRITY SHOWCASE

Each week, we invite one student to highlight his or her interests and achievements in our Celebrity Showcase. To demonstrate what we would like students to share about themselves, teachers are showcased in the first week of school. We write autobiographies and bring in pictures of ourselves and our childhood toys. Our students really enjoy learning about us and seeing pictures from when we were their age. So when it's their turn, they're extra inspired!

—*Susan Moore and Kathy Ereno*
San Jose, CA

& HAPPY ENDINGS

"What Should You Do?"

At the beginning of the school year, I help kids learn how to handle difficult social situations by having them act them out. I begin by writing down scenarios on note cards and putting them in a hat. For example, "You and a friend are sitting at a table working on a project that's due the next day. Your friend starts talking loudly and fiddling around. What should you do?" I put kids into groups of four, and each group picks one note card. They then discuss how to deal with the problem. Groups practice role-playing the situations for ten minutes, and then perform them for the class. When they are finished, we sit as a group and talk about the problems and possible solutions. Throughout the year, I have noticed many students putting the solutions we discussed into action.

—Jane Murphy
San Jose, CA

CHAIN REACTION

We've started a chain reaction of compliments in our classroom. Whenever another teacher, the principal, librarian, or a guest compliments our class, I write that person's name, the date, and what they said on a strip of construction paper. I staple the strip into a loop. As kids get additional compliments, I add strips as interlocking links. I hang the chain from the ceiling and kids love to watch it grow! When it reaches the floor, we have a compliment party and read each link of the chain. We then start a new chain, but I keep all previous ones in storage until the end of the year. Before school ends, we connect all of our chains and see how far they reach.

—Pamela Nussbaumer
Berwick, LA

MEMORIES IN THE MAKING

To celebrate our achievements over the school year, my class enjoys making a year-end scrapbook. First, students make a list of all the units we did, field trips we took, holiday programs we staged, and goals we achieved. Each student then picks one thing from the list and creates a page filled with photos, illustrations, and descriptions of the event or topic of study. My students enjoy reflecting on the year, and the scrapbook really sparks the interest of my incoming class in September.

—Stephanie Hansgen
Zanesville, OH

Brighten Up Birthdays

As a quick activity at the beginning of the year, I ask students to line themselves up in chronological order according to their birthdays. The trick is that no one may talk. Instead, students write their birthdays on slips of paper and arrange themselves from youngest to oldest. Next, I collect the slips of paper, which are now organized by date, and I mark the birthdays down on our classroom calendar. We then create a "sunshine committee" to check the calendar each month. Committee members log on to **http://dmarie.com/asp/history.asp** (a Web site that lists important events for "this day in history"). They type in students' birthdays, print out famous events from those days, and distribute the pages to students on their birthdays. Kids enjoy this recognition—and their link to history.

—Chris Thompson
Lynden, WA

A Blast from the Past

I plan a year-end surprise for students that's well worth the wait. On the last day of school each year, I ask my first-graders to draw self-portraits and to write sentences that begin, "When I graduate from high school, I want to . . ." They then paste the drawings, sentences, and their school photos on construction-paper cards. I collect the cards—and store them for 11 years! Then, a few days before these students don their caps and gowns as high-school graduates, I ask their principal to distribute the cards to students. (You could modify this activity to give cards to kids when they leave elementary school.) Students are always surprised by this "blast from the past."

—Debbie Sweatman
Gallatin, MO

5

A+ activities

GETTING YOUR

"Shoe" Papers Away

Organization is an important part of every classroom, but there isn't always enough space for storage. I've found a replacement for bulky file folders—hanging shoe bags! Papers file neatly inside the pouches which I label with students' names. The shoe bags take up very little space in my room. At the end of the week, papers are all sorted and ready to go home!

—*Darlene Parks*
Troy, VA

All Present and Accounted For

I came up with a time-saving way to take attendance and pair up students randomly. I wrote the name of each student on a tongue depressor and placed the sticks in a shoe box next to the doorway. On their way into class in the morning, each student takes his or her stick from the shoe box and places it in a decorated soup can. At a glance, I can see who's absent. Throughout the day, whenever I want students to work in pairs, I ask each to draw a partner's stick from the can.

—*Judy Bell Carlton*
Shorewood, WI

Handy Dandy

I got tired of running back and forth to my desk and shelves to get materials that I needed. To solve the problem, I bought a handy-dandy tool belt to hold all of my "teacher tools." Now crayons, markers, glue, scissors, and pencils are right there when I need them!

—*Tony Nichols*
Richwood, WV

I turned taking attendance and ordering lunch into a learning experience. My attendance chart is a bar graph that I created on the door of a metal cabinet. Each morning, students move a magnetic tag with their name onto the bar graph to indicate whether they would like to order lunch or if they packed lunch. I can instantly tell which students are absent and how many lunches to order. During class, I ask questions about the graph, such as how many more people buy lunch than pack lunch, and which column has the least amount of tags.

—*Kim Ulliman*
New Carlisle, OH

Sort It Out!

Here's a timesaving organizational tip. I use a "sorter" that I bought at an office supply store to get my students' papers in alphabetical order—instantly! At the beginning

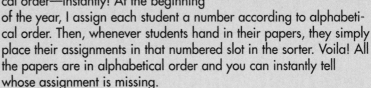

of the year, I assign each student a number according to alphabetical order. Then, whenever students hand in their papers, they simply place their assignments in that numbered slot in the sorter. Voila! All the papers are in alphabetical order and you can instantly tell whose assignment is missing.

—*Mike Zimmerman*
Naperville, IL

CHECK THE BOOK!

On the first day of school, each of my students receives an assignment book. I also have my own which I keep in the front of the classroom. Whenever I assign homework, I ask students to write the assignment in their books—and I write it down in mine. When a child returns from being absent, he or she knows to go straight to the class book and copy down missed homework. This trick has cut down on questions about assignments and encourages students to independently find out what they have missed while they were away.

—*Tracey Compton*
Dawsonville, GA

CLASS ORGANIZED

Catalog by Color

I devised a simple way to organize our extensive classroom library. Each book has a color-coded sticker on the cover that corresponds to a category, such as dark green for "animal stories." Titles are stacked in bins by category, and students are welcome to check them out anytime. They fill out the card that's in the pocket pasted to the inside cover of the book. Then they place it in the pocket on the wall chart that corresponds to their pre-assigned number. The system works great! And kids love to post book reviews on the adjacent bulletin board.

—*Jeannie DeRosa*
Huntington Beach, CA

"Choice Time" Pocket Chart

When I rewarded students with "choice time," two things used to happen: children would either vie for the same space or materials, or get into a rut, always choosing the same activity. To solve both problems, I devised a choice-time chart. First, I made a pocket chart with pictures of all the available activities. Then I created a card for each student with his or her name and picture. Now, when I randomly call out students' names and ask them to choose activities, they place their cards in the place they want to be! It's a fair, organized system that works wonders.

— *Kathy Schlief*
San Jose, CA

Staying on Schedule

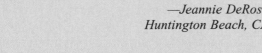

"What time is math?" "What time is lunch?" I used to hear choruses of these questions throughout the day until I came up with a solution. I made a sign for each activity or subject, including math, reading, and lunch. I then used construction paper to make analog and digital clocks that display the times these activities begin. I posted the clocks on a bulletin board along with photographs of students doing each activity and notes about the day's assignments. Now, instead of coming to me or to classmates to ask questions about what they should be doing at a certain time, kids simply glance at the bulletin board. It's cut down on disruptions, and transitioning from one activity to another runs more smoothly.

—*Kitt Langehennig*
Austin, TX

Dynamo Database

At the start of the school year, I set up a database of information about students in my class using software programs like *Access, FileMaker Pro,* or the mail-merge option in my word-processing program. The information includes birth dates, parents' names, addresses, phone numbers, e-mail addresses, and even bus numbers. I access this database whenever I need information about a student, and it saves me a lot of time especially when I'm sending letters home to parents and setting up parent/teacher conferences.

—*Patty Vreeland*
Newport News, VA

The Right Sites

To guide my students to appropriate and educational Web sites during computer time, I've created my own Internet card catalog. I write one URL (Web site address) on a card, laminate it, and file it by subject in a shoe box. Before students log on to the Internet, they pick a card from the box and visit the site that's listed. This way I know that they're logging on to sites I've approved.

—*VaReane Heese*
Omaha, NE

A+ Activities SOUNDS LIKE . . .

WHY WE LIKE THIS ACTIVITY

Onomatopoeic words are fun, expressive, and add music to poetry. They motivate students to write poetry and encourage the development of listening skills.

I introduce students to onomatopoeia by reading this poem I wrote. Then I ask students to make up stories using words and word combinations like *thwack, pitter patter, buzz, slurp, squeak, creak, rat-a-tat-tat, clink-clank, swoosh, splash, whiz, swish,* and *ticktock*. Next I ask kids to close their eyes and listen to the sounds they hear, such as paper rustling, a pencil being sharpened, and footsteps in the hall. I challenge them to make up words that imitate these sounds. Whew! Kids get really creative!

—*Diane ZuHone Shore*
Marietta, GA

- Onomatopoeia!
  How it titillates the ear
  Just listen as it imitates
  the sounds we love to hear.

- It's the vroom vroom of the engine
  and the beep beep of the horn
  It's the sizzle sizzle of the bacon
  and the pop! pop! pop! of corn.

- The clickety-clack on the railroad tracks
  and choo choo of the train
  It's the rumble of the thunder
  and the drip drop of the rain.

ADAPTING UP OR DOWN

FOR YOUNGER GRADES

Read the poem aloud to younger students and discuss the meaning of difficult vocabulary words in the first stanza, such as titillates (excites) and imitates (copies). Make sure that students understand the meaning of onomatopoeia (i.e., creating words that sound like they mean). Have students brainstorm other onomatopoeic words and list them on chart paper. Select some of the words on the list and have students share ideas about things that make those sounds. For example, whoosh could be the sound cars make passing on the highway or the sound of a vacuum-packed jar being opened.

FOR OLDER GRADES

Have students make their own lists of onomatopoeic words and then share as a class and discuss. Each child should keep a complete list to use in future writing activities.

TAKING IT FURTHER

Read a variety of age-appropriate poems that use onomatopoeia. The poetry anthology *Good Night, Sleep Tight* compiled by Ivan and Mal Jones (Scholastic, 2000) has several, including "Into the Bathtub" by Wendy Cope, "Bedtime Riddle" by Mick Gowar, "What's That?" by John Foster, "Sounds" by Peter Dixon, and "Sampan" by Tao Lang Pee. Jack Prelutsky's *It's Raining Pigs & Noodles* (Greenwillow, 2000) also includes some poems with great onomatopoeia, such as "Noisy, Noisy," "I'm Roaring Like a Lion," and "Burp!" As you read these poems to students, have them find the examples of onomatopoeia and write these onomatopoeic words on a chart. Encourage children to use the words on the chart to compose their own onomatopoeic poems. For older students share onomatopoeic poems such as Ernest Lawrence Thayer's "Casey at the Bat" and then have students write their own .

CURRICULUM CONNECTIONS

SCIENCE: Dancing Sugar

YOU'LL NEED: large metal tin, plastic wrap, large rubber band, brown sugar, cookie sheet, wooden spoon

Ask students how sound is made. Explain that sound is caused by vibrations. Define a vibration as a fast back-and-forth motion. Have students think of things that vibrate. For example, strings on a guitar vibrate when they are strummed. Rubber bands on a shoe box vibrate when they are plucked. You hear sounds because air moves, too. As the guitar or shoe box vibrates, it pushes the air around it. In this way the sound is sent through the air and reaches your ears. Your ears send nerve signals to the brain which interprets the sounds.

Although you can't see sound waves you can see their effect with the following activity.

Create a drum by stretching a piece of plastic wrap over a large round tin and securing the plastic with a rubber band. Spread a coating of brown sugar over the plastic wrap. Hold a cookie sheet close to the drum and strike it with a wooden spoon. When you bang the cookie sheet, the metal vibrates and vibrates the air around it. As this vibrating air hits the head of the drum, it makes the sugar dance!

SCIENCE: Playing With Pitch

YOU'LL NEED: several bottles, water, metal spoon

Explain that pitch is the frequency (per second) with which vibrations reach the ear. When many vibrations hit the ear in one second a high-pitched sound is created. When the number of vibrations decreases the pitch becomes lower.

To experiment with pitch, set up several bottles filled with different amounts of water at a learning center. Have children predict which bottle will have the highest (and the lowest) pitch as they blow air across the top or tap a spoon against the side. The shorter the air column (more water), the higher the pitch. Why? Each air molecule in the bottle with the largest amount of water receives a bigger share of the energy, causing it to vibrate faster. For additional hands-on science activities, see Resources.

SCIENCE: Vibrations Get Around

Have older students predict if vibrations travel faster through air, water, or solids. Suggest they construct an experiment to test their prediction.

RESOURCES

BOOKS

Kids' Poems: Teaching Kindergartners to Love Writing Poetry by Regie Routman (Scholastic, 2000). Routman has written three other books in this series geared toward first-, second-, and third- and fourth-graders.

It's Raining Pigs & Noodles by Jack Prelutsky, illustrated by James Stevenson (Greenwillow, 2000).

Good Night, Sleep Tight: A Poem for Every Night of the Year, compiled by Ivan and Mal Jones (Scholastic, 2000).

Bangs and Twangs: Science Fun With Sound by Vicki Cobb, illustrated by Steve Haefele (Millbrook, 2000).

WEB SITES

SOUND ACTIVITIES
www.exploratorium.edu/scienceexplorer/can.html Learn how to make music from a discarded can.

ONOMATOPOEIA SITES
www.amug.org/~brems/Onomatopoeia.html Read an onomatopoeic poem about a leaky faucet.

www.tnellen.com/cybereng/lit_terms/onomatopoeia.html Check out this site explaining onomatopoeia.

MEETING THE STANDARDS

STANDARDS FOR THE ENGLISH LANGUAGE ARTS

Students apply a wide range of strategies to comprehend, interpret, evaluate, and appreciate texts.

A+ activities

SIDEWALK SONNETS

WHY WE LIKE THIS ACTIVITY

Who doesn't like going outside on a nice day? It's a nice break for teachers and students and there's something indefinably delightful about using colored chalk to write outside for all to see.

As summer approaches, my students are eager to get out and enjoy the sunshine, so I take them outside to write "sidewalk sonnets." On the playground, children write verses about the end of school or summer with colored chalk. When finished, each student reads his or her poem to the class. This activity inspires even the most reluctant writers and requires no cleanup!

—Pamela Schmieder
Zanesville, OH

ADAPTING UP OR DOWN

FOR YOUNGER GRADES

Have students close their eyes and summon up summer sights, sounds, tastes, and feelings. Encourage children to share their favorite "senses" of summer. Have each child contribute a word that tells about why he or she loves summer. Write all the words on chart paper. Next, have each child think up a word that rhymes with his or her first word and add to the chart paper. For example, children might think up rhyming pairs such as fireflies/french fries, barbecue/morning dew, and so on. Then take the class outside. With colored chalk write *Why we love summer . . .* onto the surface of the playground. Have children write their rhyming pairs together in the form of a poem and illustrate them. Read the collaborative class poem and enjoy the warm weather!

FOR OLDER GRADES

Explain that sonnets are 14-line poems with several possible rhyme schemes. The rhyme scheme for an English sonnet is *abab cdcd efef gg*. Read students examples of sonnets with this rhyme scheme and then take students out on the playground to write their own in colored chalk. Share poems and discuss different feelings about summer.

RESOURCES

BOOKS
Hopscotch Around the World by Mary D. Lankford, illustrated by Karen Milone (Beech Tree, 1996).

CDs
Chants by Katherine Dines (Hunk-Ta-Bunk-Ta, 2001).

WEB SITES
www.junebox.com Log on to order a U.S.A. or world map kit.

MEETING THE STANDARDS

STANDARDS FOR THE ENGLISH LANGUAGE ARTS

Students employ a wide range of strategies as they write and use different writing process elements appropriately to communicate with different audiences for a variety of purposes.

TAKING IT FURTHER

*S*imple songs and chants are heard on playgrounds everywhere. Encourage your students to develop and extend this oral tradition. Ask students to volunteer chants they are familiar with and explain how and when they use them. Some children may volunteer a jump-rope rhyme such as "Teddy Bear." Others may suggest a song such as "London Bridge."

Chant one of these rhymes with children drawing their attention to the number of beats to a measure. Let students clap the beats as you chant together. Then have students substitute the traditional words to one of these rhymes with words about summer, keeping the same rhythm and rhyme pattern. Take students outside and have them write their new rhymes onto the playground with colored chalk. Take turns singing each student's summertime chant.

CURRICULUM CONNECTIONS

MATH: Math in Motion
YOU'LL NEED: playground surface or butcher paper, colored chalk or markers

Take students outside and, using sidewalk chalk, construct number lines (1-10 or 1-100, depending on students' ages and intended activities). You can also do this activity in the gym, cafeteria, or another large space. Spread pieces of butcher paper and use markers to create number lines.

You can do a multitude of math activities with playground number lines. Here are just a few suggestions to get you started. Have students hop on all the odd or even numbers, or on all the odd and even numbers between two numbers, say between 50 and 100. Let students hop on numbers as they count by *twos*, *threes*, *fives*, and so on. Students can also use the number line to add, subtract, multiply, and divide. For example, "Mark, stand on the number that is the quotient of $100 \div 10$," or give Jamie a sum, such as 12 and instruct her to hop on two numbers that add up to that number, such as 5 and 7.

creative classroom

GEOGRAPHY: Making a United States/World Map
YOU'LL NEED: Colored chalk, playground surface
Optional: U.S.A. Map Stencil Kit or World Map Stencil Kit with paint (see Resources, left)

Using either a stencil or drawing freehand, create a United States or world map on the playground. Have children write in the names of states or countries, and add towns, cities, important landforms, bodies of water, landmarks, and so on. Then use the map to play geography games. For example, give each child a card with a state's name on it. Call out a capital city or landmark and have the child who holds the state in which that capital or landmark is located stand on that state on the map. Then use the compass rose to teach directions: Ask students to stand northeast of the capital, southwest of the landmark, and so forth.

PHYSICAL EDUCATION/SOCIAL STUDIES:
Just a Hop Skip and Jump Away
YOU'LL NEED: playground surface, colored chalk

After a discussion about games that are played worldwide, such as jacks, marbles, and hopscotch, explain that the rules, equipment, and names may vary, but the games are basically the same. Then illustrate with the following French version of hopscotch called *Escargot*, the French word for snail.

Share with students that the hopscotch pattern in Escargot is shaped like the spiral of a snail shell. It is drawn in chalk on the playground and the boxes in the pattern are numbered 1 through 17. Then divide your class into groups of four and take them outside to duplicate the snail pattern. Review the following rules and have students demonstrate.

1. Players decide on which foot they will hop. 2. The first player hops through the pattern towards the center, hopping into every box on the same foot. (If a player steps on or outside the lines, it is the next player's turn.) Once he or she hops into the center space, this player can now rest, with both feet on the ground. 3. The player then turns around to follow the pattern back. If successful, the player must then repeat the pattern once more. If not successful, the next player goes. 4. If a player has successfully hopped through the pattern twice, he or she may pick a "house" by writing his or her initials in one space with chalk. This "house" becomes a rest space for only this player. All other players must hop over it. 5. As the game continues, more of the squares become "houses," marked with players' initials. It then becomes too difficult for any of the players to hop into the center space. The game then ends and the player with the most "houses" wins.

A NOTEWORTHY IDEA

A+ activities

WHY WE LIKE THIS ACTIVITY

*G*raphic organizers are wonderful visual tools that help students see how to organize knowledge and make important connections among concepts. They require that students learn actively by providing a framework from which to attach new knowledge. And the use of sticky notes makes these visual tools manageable for even the youngest learners.

*W*hen I ask my young students to make their own story webs and concept maps, they usually end up with illegible pages filled with scrunched-up writing. To help them space out their ideas, I now give each student a stack of small sticky notes. They write one idea on each and place the notes on a sheet of paper around the central topic. They can then rearrange and add more sticky notes as they think of new ideas.

—*VaReane Heese*
Omaha, NE

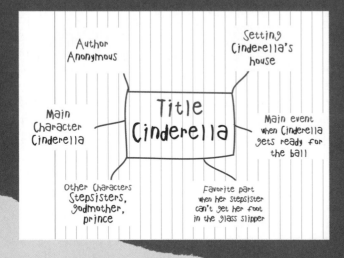

ADAPTING UP OR DOWN

FOR YOUNGER GRADES

*A*sk primary students to each list one event in the plot of a book you are reading. Provide sticky notes for their answers. (Have prereaders illustrate their ideas or dictate them to you.) Then group all the sticky notes together on an easel or chart paper, discarding duplicates. With children's help, start organizing the events in the order in which they took place, forming a vertical time line. Then ask students if any parts of the plot are missing. Have them tell you where to add these events in the overall order. Then review all events from first to last.

FOR OLDER GRADES

*G*ive older students a mixed-up list of events from a plot sequence. Have students put these events on sticky notes and then identify the climax or "turning point" in the plot. Then ask them to arrange all the events in order, building up from the introduction to the climax and descending from the climax to the resolution.

Climax

Introduction   **Resolution**

MEETING THE STANDARDS

STANDARDS FOR THE ENGLISH LANGUAGE ARTS
*S*tudents use spoken, written, and visual language to accomplish their own purposes (e.g., for learning, enjoyment, persuasion, and the exchange of information).

TAKING IT FURTHER

AN ASSORTMENT OF ORGANIZERS

*I*ntroduce and illustrate different types of graphic organizers: *hierarchical, conceptual, sequential,* and *cyclical.*

A **hierarchical organizer** has a pattern that includes one main concept and sub-concepts.

A **conceptual organizer** has a pattern consisting of a *central idea* with s*upporting facts.* Inform students that these organizers are used for describing something or someone, listing solutions to a problem, or comparing and contrasting information. A Venn diagram, which has two overlapping circles, is a type of conceptual organizer that shows information being compared and contrasted.

Graphic organizers that arrange events in order are known as **sequential organizers.** Share that sequential organizers are appropriate to use when organizing events with a specific beginning and end. A time line is an example of a sequential organizer.

1 yr	2 yrs	3 yrs	4 yrs	5 yrs	6 yrs	7 yrs
learned to walk	learned to talk	got first tricycle	in preschool	in kinder-garten	first sleepover	in second grade

The **cyclical organizer** describes a series of events within a process. Explain that there is no beginning or end—just a sequence of continuous events, such as the seasons of the year.

CURRICULUM CONNECTIONS

SCIENCE, SOCIAL STUDIES, MATH: Picking a Pattern

*D*ivide the class into small groups. Assign each group one of the following topics or a topic of your own choosing to illustrate with a graphic organizing pattern. Have groups share their different types of organizers.

✔ How a tadpole becomes a frog

✔ How a rectangle and a square are alike/different

✔ Give facts supporting the main idea that spring/summer/fall/winter is the best season.

✔ How a tomato seed becomes a tomato

✔ How a bill becomes a law

✔ How to make change from a dollar

✔ Order events leading up to the Civil War

✔ Compare and contrast different types of families in a community

RESOURCES

WEB SITES
For teachers

www.inspiration.com View lessons using *Inspiration* and *Kidspiration* concept-mapping software.

www.graphic.org/goindex.html Log on to learn about various types of organizers and when to use them.

BOOKS

Graphic Organizers: Visual Strategies for Active Learning by Karen Bromley, Linda Irwin-De Vitis, and Marcia Modlo (Scholastic, 1995).

Webbing with Literature: Creating Story Maps with Children's Books by Karen Bromley (Allyn & Bacon, 1991).

Prereading Activities for Content Area Reading and Learning (International Reading Association, 1989).

SOFTWARE
For students

Kidspiration from Inspiration Software
Mac/Windows CD-ROM
(800) 877-4292
www.inspiration.com

Timeliner from Tom Snyder Productions
Mac/Windows CD-ROM
(800) 342-0236
www.teachtsp.com

creative
classroom

CHARACTER THOUGHTS

A+ activities

WHY WE LIKE THIS ACTIVITY

This critical-thinking activity encourages readers to "connect" with characters in books. By delving into characters' feelings, students can draw conclusions about their thoughts and actions.

I encourage my students to get into the thoughts of the characters in the books we read. They begin by working in groups. Each group draws a life-sized picture of one of the book's characters. Then they make "thought bubbles" in which they write what they believe the character is thinking in the story. We then staple the characters and their thought bubbles to a bulletin board. Reading other students' ideas about what the characters are thinking motivates my students to continue reading and encourages them to discuss the book with their friends.

—Becky Hetz
Waterford, PA

ADAPTING UP OR DOWN

FOR YOUNGER GRADES

Select a story, such as *Corduroy* by Don Freeman, for whole-class guided reading. On a large sheet of chart paper, draw three silhouettes of Corduroy the Bear with "thought bubbles." As you read the story aloud, ask students the following questions: *What is Corduroy thinking when Lisa's mom will not let her buy the bear? . . . when he is in the store looking for his button? . . . when Lisa is sewing Corduroy's button on to his overalls?* Write student responses inside each of the thought bubbles. After reading, have students write thought bubbles for other characters in the story.

FOR OLDER GRADES

While reading a novel or chapter book, have students write thought bubbles for each character during specific events, such as the beginning, climax, and end of the story. Have them discuss whether or not the character's feelings towards someone or something have changed and why. Then group students to write scripts for specific scenes or chapters in the book. Suggest they use a narrator to reveal the thoughts of each character and incorporate them into their scenes. Have students attach yardsticks to the backs of the life-sized characters and use them as props when performing their skits.

MEETING THE STANDARDS

NATIONAL COUNCIL OF TEACHERS OF ENGLISH
English Language Arts Standard
Students apply a wide range of strategies to comprehend, interpret, evaluate, and appreciate texts.

TAKING IT FURTHER

CHARACTER CONVERSATIONS

*A*fter students have read several selections and created cut-outs, have them consider what kind of dialogue might exist between characters from different stories. For example, using the novels *Lyddie* by Katherine Paterson and *Out of the Dust* by Karen Hesse, prompt students by asking: *If Lyddie, living in Lowell, Massachusetts in 1843, was to write to Billie Jo, living in the Oklahoma Panhandle during the Great Depression, what advice would she give her?* Pair students with kids from another class and have them write letters back and forth. Encourage them to share letters and write situation cartoons with "dialogue bubbles."

DEAR DIARY

*B*efore reading a novel, have kids design a book journal. As they read the novel, have them role-play by writing diary entries for one of the characters. Have kids include such things as feelings about events in the story or other characters. For example, in the story *Roll of Thunder, Hear My Cry*, Cassie Logan's journal might discuss her feelings towards the Wallace boys, the burning of her home, and the desire to end racism. The journal entries might also include the character's predictions about how the story will end.

CREATIVE CUTOUTS

*H*ave kids cut out pictures of people, animals, or objects from magazines and newspapers. Then have them glue the pictures onto pieces of construction paper. Have kids write about what they think is happening in each scene. Challenge kids to stretch their thinking and create "thought bubbles" for the people, animals, or objects. Guide them by linking human qualities to the cutouts of animals and objects. Ask questions such as: *What kind of attitude do you think a luxury car has? What do you think a refrigerator might be thinking? What brands of litter do cats prefer?*

WHO THOUGHT THAT?

*M*otivate students to study for an upcoming exam or end-of-the-year review. List stories, passages, and novels the entire class has read. Then write down a thought or statement representing each of the major characters from these assignments. Write each thought/statement on an individual strip of paper (and include the character's name and the title of the book or story). Use the strips as clues in an identification game called "Who Thought That?" Divide the class into teams and read aloud the "thought clues." Have kids name the character who "thought that" as well as the book or story title.

CURRICULUM CONNECTIONS

SOCIAL STUDIES: The Life and Times of . . .
YOU'LL NEED: various age-appropriate biographies of historical figures

Assign students to read a biography of a historical figure. Then encourage them to "get into character" and pretend they are the historical figure accepting an award or receiving a great honor. Have students write a monologue or speech from this person's point of view. During pre-writing, guide kids to focus on the person's thoughts about an important issue or a major event from the time period in which they lived. Encourage students to enhance their presentations by dressing in period clothing or creating period props from household items.

RESOURCES

WEB SITE
www.education-world.com/a_sites/sites021.shtml Explore these useful links when teaching about biographies.

BOOKS
Corduroy by Don Freeman (Illustrator, 1976).

Lyddie by Katherine Paterson (Puffin, 1994).

Out of the Dust by Karen Hesse (Scholastic, 1999).

Roll of Thunder, Hear My Cry by Mildred Taylor (Puffin, 1991).

A+ activities

STUDENT-CREATED

I found a way to ensure that kids take our quarterly newsletter home to parents—by asking students to write it themselves! I make a list of activities that the class has engaged in during the last several weeks. Each student chooses a topic and reports on it, often interviewing other students and teachers. After the students type, spell check, and proofread their articles on our class computers, we import clip art. I paste all the articles into a final document and print. The newsletters make it home because students are excited to share their work.

—*Diane Landry*
Mesa, AZ

Trash Day a Big Success

Mrs Jones's 5th-grade class had a big clean-up day last Friday. Students banded together in teams and tried to see which team could pick up more trash.

Team One, which was made up of Billy W., Janice R., Jamal T. and Caitlin S., got the most points. The winning team got to start the ECO-BOARD, a bulletin board in the classroom that keeps track of everything the class does to help the planet. We all agreed that our cleanup day will become a class tradition.

WHY WE LIKE THIS ACTIVITY

*T*his activity provides a real-life purpose for nonfiction writing. Students are encouraged to write well and include accurate information for a wide audience. The newsletters also encourage students to review concepts they have learned and foster a school-home connection.

ADAPTING UP OR DOWN

FOR YOUNGER GRADES

*H*ave students write a class summary whenever they complete a major project or there is an important classroom event. Ask them to reflect on the project with questions such as: *What steps did we do during this project? What did you learn? What did you like best about it?* Write students' responses on separate strips of paper. As a class, work together to arrange the sentences to make a coherent description of the project, and ask students to fill in any missing details. Type all the sentences into a document, and save it to include in your next class newsletter.

FOR OLDER GRADES

*H*ave students "apply" for various jobs on the newsletter (features editor, sports writer, theater critic, cartoonist, photographer, etc.) by completing applications and writing resumes. Place students in departments according to their interests and abilities. Have them work in teams to develop a focus for story ideas and to write and edit articles.

MEETING THE STANDARDS

STANDARDS FOR THE ENGLISH LANGUAGE ARTS

*S*tudents adjust their use of spoken, written, and visual language to communicate effectively with a variety of audiences and for different purposes. Students conduct research on issues and interests by generating ideas and questions, and by posing problems. They gather, evaluate, and synthesize data from a variety of sources to communicate their discoveries in ways that suit their purpose and audience.

NEWSLETTER

TAKING IT FURTHER

GET INTO THE INTERVIEW

*P*repare students to interview people for their articles by guiding them to write appropriate questions. Ask: *What is the difference between the question 'Do you like your job?' and 'What do you like about your job?'"* (The first is a yes/no question, while the second is open-ended.) Encourage students to develop open-ended questions that use the five W's: who, what, where, when, why, (and how). List sample questions on chart paper and ask students to order them logically. Also, offer students note-taking tips. To model interviewing skills, show videotapes of television interviews. Ask students to practice interviewing each other using open-ended questions.

RESOURCES

WEB SITES

www.boondocksnet.com/gallery/pc_intro.html Log on for links to historical political cartoons and cartoonists.
http://cagle.slate.msn.com This site has numerous examples of current political cartoons.
www–ed.fnal.gov/linc/fall95/projects/butcher/Internetproject 2.html Access a lesson about creating a newspaper.

BOOKS

Create Your Own Class Newspaper: A Complete Guide for Planning, Writing, and Publishing a Newspaper by Diane Crosby (Incentive, 1995).

Kids in Print: Publishing a School Newspaper by Mark Levin (Good Apple, 1997).

The Young Journalist's Book: How to Write and Produce Your Own Newspaper by Donna Guthrie and Nancy Bentley (Millbrook, 1998).

SOFTWARE

Classroom Newspaper Workshop (Tom Snyder Productions). Call (800) 342-0236 or visit www.teachtsp.com

Knockout Newsletters (Creative Teaching Press). Call (800) 287-8879 or visit www.creativeteaching.com

CURRICULUM CONNECTIONS

ART/SOCIAL STUDIES: Political Cartoons
YOU'LL NEED: paper, pencils, erasers, current newspapers, examples of political cartoons

A picture is worth a thousand words—and so is a political cartoon. From the facial features the artist exaggerates and the choice of words, a reader can infer the artist's opinion on an issue. Show students examples of political cartoons (see Resources, left). Even if they do not understand the political issue, they will be able to draw some conclusions. Ask students to focus on the features and objects that stand out. Do the people have large ears? Are they holding, throwing, sitting on, or ignoring anything? List students' observations on one side of chart paper. Then ask students to interpret the possible messages the illustrator is portraying through these features and objects. Have students choose a local, national, or historical news topic and design a political cartoon to represent their opinion of the issue.

SOCIAL STUDIES:
Old News Can Be Good News!
YOU'LL NEED: paper, pencils, resources on history or ancient cultures

Help students bring history and ancient cultures to life by having them make a historical newspaper. They can "interview" Thomas Jefferson after the signing of the Declaration of Independence, report on the progress of building the Egyptian pyramids, or draw a political cartoon about the problems that will arise because of the "new" invention of the telephone. Use the following Candlewick Press books as references: *The Aztec News* by Philip Steele, *The Roman News* by Andrew Langley, *The Egyptian News* by Scott Steedman, *The Greek News* by Anton Powell, and *The Viking News* by Rachel Wright. Another excellent resource is the Newspaper Histories Series from EDC Publications, which includes *Medieval Messenger, Egyptian Echo, Roman Record*, and *Stone Age Sentinel*. Young students can do similar "news reporting" on famous fairy tales or children's stories, e.g., "Pigs' House Blown Down by Wolf!"

READING NOOKS

Rub-a-Dub Literature

To inspire our emergent readers to dive into books, we created an irresistible reading nook. We asked an area business to donate an old tub, painted it fire-engine red, and filled it with comfy pillows, books, and puppets. Now pairs of children can grab a book, jump in the tub, and brush up on reading skills, using the puppets to act out the story. Nearby, we hang kid-created

big books from a reading tree, so students can take their own work into the tub. It's made a big splash in our classroom.

—*Kathy Lane and Bronwyn McLemore*
Jacksonville, FL

Get Psyched for Summer Reading

To encourage children to read during the upcoming summer vacation, I created a reading nook that says, "Welcome to the great outdoors—indoors." It's a tent that sets the mood for the summer with the help of a battery-operated Coleman lantern and a tree with "fireflies" (a string of small white lights).

—*Cindy McFall*
Seymour, TN

Like a Day at the Beach

As summer approaches, I teach my students that reading time can be like a day at the beach. Students don sunglasses and flip flops and kick back in beach chairs. It's a way to remind them that while they're having fun in the sun, they can also learn.

—*Carol Deets*
Mountainside, NJ

A *TREE*MENDOUS IDEA

If you look closely at the student in my rainforest reading center, you'll notice that she is sitting on a stump. I asked a local gardening company to take a big tree they had cut down and chop it up into blocks. Kids, knock on wood, love to sit on them when they read. And by completing the rainforest "look," the stumps make our center a magical place.

—*Kathy Kronemeyer*
Indio, CA

BOOKS ON WHEELS

To get my fourth-graders on a roll with reading, I placed two tires in our book nook that were donated by a local car dealer. I painted them with bright colors and stuffed the holes with pillows. Now my students never tire of reading!

—*Heather Mitchell*
Hallandale, Fl.

Our Reading Goal

For Children's Book Week (in November), I kick off a six-week reading incentive program with my third-graders by literally creating a reading "goal." I make a reading nook that looks like a soccer goal out of plastic pipes, twist ties, pipe cleaners, and inexpensive netting, and I place artificial grass beneath it. When students finish a project early or have independent reading time, I invite them to grab a book, sit inside the goal, and score! I write the name of each book that students finish on a paper "soccer ball" and post it behind the goal. At the end of six weeks, we give a cheer for all the reading we've done.

—*Sheryl T. Piper*
Sulphur, LA

COZY CORNER

Make reading a reward. Bring in an easy chair. When students accomplish something special, award them five minutes in the chair to sit and read.

—*Nancy Kim*
New York, NY

creative classroom

ILLUSTRATION: ANDY LEVINE

MOTIVATING

Wordless Picture Books

I've found a way for upper-grade students to reinforce reading comprehension skills and teach about literature to kindergarten buddies. After fifth- and sixth-graders read a novel, such as *The Lion, the Witch, and the Wardrobe,* they make a story map by selecting scenes that are critical to the plot and illustrating them. Each illustration depicts the main idea of the scene as well as supporting details. They bind the illustrations together in a book and include a plot summary on the last page. Children use the illustrated book to "read" the novel to their kinderbuddies.

—*Sue Neeley*
Steubenville, OH

TAKE-HOME READINGS

My kindergartners (and their busy parents!) rave about my "Book-in-a-Bag" program. Every Monday, each student checks out a book for the week. We place the book in a gallon-sized freezer bag along with a bookmark, a laminated page with a few comprehension questions, and a cassette tape of me reading the story aloud—which is especially helpful for harried parents. Students enjoy sharing the books with their parents and listening to their teacher read to them at night. They've also learned responsibility. We've had to replace many bags because they've been used too much, but I haven't lost a book yet!

—*Bernadette Smith*
Jack, AL

Reading Isn't Scary

When my new crop of first-graders came to school, many were nervous about reading, and worried that they wouldn't be able to learn. To symbolize scaring their fears away—and to celebrate fall, too—we made

scarecrows by stuffing grocery bags and adding construction-paper features. We displayed our creations along with cornstalks. To culminate the activity, we read books about scarecrows and autumn.

—*Karin Huttsell*
Ft. Wayne, IN

Recruiting Readers

My students love to have guests come to our classroom to read to them. To recruit readers, I post a sign-up sheet in the teacher's lounge, and invite teachers, assistants, and support staff to sign up. Our school superintendent even participated! To remember all the readers, I take a photo of each guest with the children and display it on a bulletin board by our door. My students always look forward to seeing who the next reader will be!

—*Joan Goff*
Asheville, NC

That's the Ticket!

I found a way to motivate my students to read more. For every ten books a child reads at home—confirmed by parents' signatures—I give the child a reading ticket. I also give out tickets for turning in book-related writing assignments early, returning books to the library on time, and so on. Students can redeem reading tickets for rewards—such as having me "drop everything and read" aloud to them for five or ten minutes when the class schedule permits. In my class, reading is the ticket!

—*Debbie Crawford*
Holland, OH

CHILDREN TO READ

What were these children doing five minutes ago?

Lending Library

To bring new books into my classroom and keep my kindergartners excited about reading, I've established a unique lending library. At the beginning of the school year, a local bookstore sends me 60 new picture books on consignment. I invite parents to my classroom to purchase these books at a discount (pre-arranged with the bookstore). Any unpurchased books are returned and parents lend the books they buy to my classroom library. That way, all the students can enjoy reading the books throughout the year. In June, kids whose parents purchased books take them home. Meanwhile, the library encourages students to take care of books because they know they belong to fellow classmates.

—*Mary Anne Callaghan*
Macomb Township, MI

THOUGHT-PROVOKING PHOTOS

Creating your own story starters can be quick, easy, and inexpensive. I gather old magazines, cut out intriguing pictures, and staple them to index cards. I then write thought-provoking questions under each picture. For example, under a picture of a dog riding in a car, I ask, "Where is this dog going? Who is driving the car?" Each card is different so every student must use his or her own creative thinking to come up with an answer. In June, after a year of practice with the cards, I have my students prepare new cards for my incoming students.

—*Sonia Steiner*
Philadelphia, PA

PICTURE THIS!

Students in my remedial reading group and I created a poster to inspire them to read and share best-loved books. I took a picture of each student holding his or her favorite book. We pasted the photos on a bulletin board to form the letters R-E-A-D. Students love to see themselves in pictures, and the bulletin board inspires them to explore all the adventures found in books.

— *Wanda May*
Vaughn, WA

Be a Bookworm!

Here's a wonderful incentive for students to read independently and write about the books they've read. I made a "bookworm head" out of construction paper and hung it in the hallway. After a child has read a book, he or she writes a review of it on "bookworm paper" (a round sheet of paper with "feet" that I created). Kids then add the paper to the bookworm's body. As the bookworm grows, inching its way down the hallway, so does my students' excitement about books.

—*Denise Shaw*
Cherry Hill, NJ

THE "ART" OF READING

Here's how I help my beginning readers "read." I compose "rebus stories" on the computer. A rebus story has illustrations in place of difficult words. I replace tough words with clip-art pictures. Now all of my 👥 are 🙂 because they can read.

—*VaReane Heese*
Omaha, NE

SPIFFING UP

Student-made Grammar Guides

Lessons on punctuation and grammar can be boring, but I've found an interactive way to make learning the rules more interesting. Each time I teach a new rule, I ask students to search newspapers and magazines for examples. (For instance, if we're learning about question marks, students must locate a sentence in which a question mark is properly used.) They then cut out the example, paste it on a note card, and write the grammar rule below it. At the end of the unit, they punch holes at the tops of the cards and connect them with metal rings to make mini-books. Kids keep these reference guides in their desks and use them when proofreading their writing throughout the year.

—Rosemary Leavy
Berwyn, PA

Proofreading Presentations

To help my students practice proofreading, I tap into technology. Using *AppleWorks*, I type a humorous one-page, double-spaced story about an event in my life—and I fill it with proofreading errors. I number each line for easy reference and make a copy for each student in the class. After kids edit my story individually, we go over the corrections together by connecting my *AppleWorks* document to the classroom television so that everyone can see it. I also invite students to type their own error-ridden stories into *AppleWorks* and project them on the television screen. We then correct the errors as a class.

—Kevin Morris
Vienna, VA

Homophones in a Pair Tree

I created a bulletin board tree for my sixth-grade class to study homophone pairs. I built the tree by crunching up brown butcher paper and "having it grow" up a wall, with its branches stretching across the ceiling. I used a die-cutting machine to make maple leaves in various fall colors and wrote homophone pairs (blew, blue) or trios (too, to, two) on matching colored leaves, one word per leaf. Then I laminated them to save for another year.

At the beginning of each week I began our discussion of homophones by holding up just one leaf of each pair/trio. The students supplied the matching words and alternate spellings. They also created definitions and entered all the information on homophone study sheets in their notebooks. After we did this for each pair/trio, I hung the leaves on the tree. Then I challenged students to come up with a sentence per pair/trio that demonstrated their understanding of the different spellings and their meanings. For example: "The wind **blew** the **blue** boat across the water." The leaves remained on the tree all year, and as it filled up, the students had the pleasure of working on their reading and writing under a tree, as well as having a helpful reminder of the various spellings of same-sounding words.

—Barbara D'Elia
Austin, TX

Add the Adjective

To help my students learn parts of speech, we play the following game to practice identifying nouns and adjectives. I ask one student to silently choose something that's visible in the classroom: a noun. The child then uses adjectives to describe the mystery noun until the class guesses what it is. For example, a student might say "white," "gritty," and "powdery" to describe chalk. I find that this game encourages students to broaden their descriptive vocabularies.

—Lydia Marlow
Independence, MO

When my students write a story, they are usually so involved in getting their ideas down on paper that they forget to add adjectives. I help them paint more vivid pictures in their readers' minds with this simple technique. After they hand in their first drafts, I highlight nouns in their stories that could benefit from added adjectives. Students then revise their stories, turning "cats" into "white, fluffy cats," and "dogs" into "huge, fierce dogs."

—Nancy Y. Karpyk
Weirton, WV

SPELLING & GRAMMAR

Step on It!

Here's a hands-on—well, foots-on—way to practice spelling. I laminated 26 sheets of 8"x10" paper, one for each letter of the alphabet. I placed the letters in three rows on the floor and arranged them as if they were on a computer keyboard. Now I ask one student to call out a spelling word while another spells the word by stepping on the letters and saying them aloud. It's a fun-filled, active way for my students to learn their spelling words and the placement of letters on a keyboard!

—Leslie Gates
Albion, NY

WORD SLEUTHS

At the beginning of the school year I set up a Spelling Sleuth chart. Whenever children in my class notice a word with an unusual spelling pattern, such as a soft *c* in the word *celery*, I write it on the chart. The children then enjoy "sleuthing" for other words with soft *c*'s to add. This chart really helps take the mystery out of spelling.

—Jane Darnell
Alexandria, VA

Silly Sentences

Students in my class get a lot of laughs while learning about the parts of speech. I write words that are nouns on red index cards, verbs on blue, adverbs on yellow, adjectives on orange, and articles and prepositions on pink. Students pick one card from each category and create zany sentences. Some of the combinations are hilarious. This is a painless way for students to learn about the parts of speech and sentence construction.

—Lorraine McKay
St. Louis, MO

Jazz Up Spelling

Singing our second-grade words has made learning to spell them a snap. We sing them anytime we have a few extra minutes. Sometimes we sing the letters to a snappy beat, sometimes low "like a man," high "like a mouse," or grand "like an opera singer." The sillier, the better. The kids love it, and so do I!

— Janet Cesarini-Janik
Lake Jackson, TX

Score with Spelling

To encourage students to study for their spelling tests, we give a trial test each Wednesday—and a reward. Students who make a perfect score get a chance to guess at a secret number we've chosen between 1 and 100. The child who comes closest gives the final test to the rest of the class on Friday. The chance to become the teacher for a moment is a real incentive for students to study.

—Lori Christopoulos
and Angie Castleberry
Tulsa, OK

It's a Puzzle

I may have found a cure for spelling test boredom! Instead of simply spelling words correctly, I have students solve a crossword puzzle. It's easy with a CD-ROM program such as *Crosswords & More* (Expert Software). For clues, I provide synonyms for the week's spelling words. Kids use an online thesaurus to find the meanings and then use the spelling words to complete the puzzle. Not only are students spelling the words, they're also learning their meanings.

— Helayna Campo
North Babylon, NY

23

A+ activities

MOTIVATING

Apple Picking

Our study of Johnny Appleseed and plants each fall is highlighted by a descriptive writing project. I begin by distributing one apple to each student. Kids then write a detailed description of their apple on an index card and place the card under their apple on the table. While the children are at lunch, I mix up the apples. When they return, I randomly distribute the cards and kids use the descriptions to try to find their classmates' apples. What a way for kids to get a "taste" for good descriptive writing!

—*Virginia Dodge*
Garrison, NY

Keep in touch

To give children an incentive to practice their letter-writing skills over the summer, on the last day of school I give each student a self-addressed, stamped postcard. I promise children that if they write to me, I will write back. It's fun for me to correspond with the children I've become so fond of during the year. Parents have told me how excited their children get when they receive mail from their teacher.

—*Barbara J. Rosso*
Rock Hill, SC

Personalized "Pencils"

To motivate my students to write, I give them a permanent place to display their work. First, I cut out blank pieces of paper in the shapes of pencils. Then, kids decorate the pencil shapes with their names and drawings. We hang the "pencils" on a bulletin board, spacing them out so that we can hang a paper below each one. Students then may display their work under the "pencils," and can remove and replace it when they feel it has been read and enjoyed by their classmates. This simple board has helped my students gain pride in their work.

—*Judy Meagher*
Bozeman, MT

SUMMER "SHORT" STORIES

Students love this "short" writing activity because they can share what they did during summer vacation. I distribute 3"x 5" index cards and ask kids to write short paragraphs about their summers. They then draw a pair of short pants on construction paper, cut them out, and paste the paragraphs onto the shorts. As an eye-catching way to display the "short" stories, I clip them to a clothesline with colorful clothespins.

—*Nicole Cox*
Riverdale, MD

Lost-and-Found Stories

Taking my students to our school's overflowing lost and found provides inspiration for a year-end writing project and helps clean out the bin. As students sort through the lost and found, they retrieve lost belongings and each borrows an unclaimed article for a day. Students then create stories about how these items ended up in the lost and found. This activity piques students' creativity—and parents are happy to see missing things finally make it home.

—*Brianna Deering*
Lake Geneva, WI

CHILDREN TO WRITE

NEWSPAPERS AS MUSE

Each year, in honor of Poetry Month (April), I turn my old stacks of newspapers into a poetry center for my fifth-graders. Each student gets a newspaper, a pair of scissors, a glue stick, and a blank sheet of paper. Kids look through the newspaper and clip descriptive words and phrases from headlines or advertisements. They arrange their clippings on the sheet of paper to create a poem and then paste the clippings in place. The children are always very proud of their work!

—Martha Colella
Staten Island, NY

PEN PAL PORTRAITS

To hone their descriptive writing skills and "connect" with their Internet pen pals, my students took a long, hard look at themselves in the mirror. Then, after contemplating their features, they brainstormed adjectives to describe themselves, wrote descriptions, and e-mailed the information to their cyberspace friends. (To find an e-mail pen-pal class, try **www.epals.com/** or **www.KS-connection. org:80/penpal/penpal.html**). After receiving the e-mails, the pen pals then drew pictures of what they thought my students looked like and sent them to us via snail mail. My students were delighted at how closely the sketches matched their appearances. They can thank their writing skills for that!

—Lee Ann Olsen
Mystic, CT

See Me on TV!

To encourage my students to write, I videotape them reading their own work. We then broadcast the video across the school during video announcements. Seeing themselves on television is a great incentive for kids to write well.

—Kimberly S. Conway
Manassas, VA

SUPERPOWERS

Have students imagine that they can be empowered with one superhuman ability, such as X-ray vision or superhuman strength. Ask: *What power would you possess and how would you use it?* Have students translate this information into an adventure story.

—Eileen Liebes
Jersey City, NJ

"Hats On" to Writing!

My students wear many "hats" throughout the day. They especially love the author's top hats, bonnets, and berets they made from inexpensive party hats I purchased for each student. Kids decorate their hats with markers, magazine pictures, stickers, and other decorations that inspire them to write. They don their hats when they need to overcome writer's block and as they read their work aloud while sitting in our writer's chair. Hats off to this activity because it inspires even the most reluctant students to write.

—Elyse Moore
Dallas, TX

An Imaginary Point of View

To practice their point-of-view skills, my students enter the land of make-believe. I pair each of my second-graders with a buddy in a third-grade class. Pairs then correspond with one another as if they were fairy-tale characters at odds. For example, if a student pretends to be one of the "three little pigs," he or she writes to "the big bad wolf." Then the wolf responds to the pig's letter. I then have children swap roles so that they get practice writing from different points of view.

—Mary Bolte
Mansfield, OH

THE ART OF MATH

WHY WE LIKE THIS ACTIVITY

This activity provides a real-world connection between two subjects that are often taught separately: art and math. By encouraging students to notice shapes in artwork and objects, students learn to look beyond the obvious. They are then challenged to "see as Picasso saw things" by translating a picture from their textbooks into geometric shapes.

To extend my geometry lessons, I show students examples of how Pablo Picasso used shapes in his paintings. As a class, we identify the shapes in Picasso's *Three Musicians* and then recreate the picture using only geometric figures. Later, students try the same technique on their own to copy Picasso's *Boy in Sailor Suit with Butterfly Net* and pictures from their textbooks.

—*Debra Peterson*
San Ysidro, CA

ADAPTING UP OR DOWN

FOR YOUNGER GRADES

When showing students Picasso's *Three Musicians* or another painting, hold up construction paper shapes (a square, circle, rectangle, triangle, etc.) and ask students to find the same shapes in the painting. When they locate one, ask a student to trace it with his or her finger. Then invite students to locate another example of the same shape and compare them (e.g., "Which is larger?" "Are they different colors?" "Are they turned around?"). Continue this procedure with each shape in the painting.

FOR OLDER GRADES

Ask students to work in pairs to identify the shapes in Picasso's painting and discuss their similarities and differences. Then bring the class together to compare findings.

CURRICULUM CONNECTIONS

SCIENCE: Geometric Nature Walk
YOU'LL NEED: camera, pencils, paper, erasers
To extend this geometry lesson, head outdoors on a nature walk. Take a camera or invite students to bring sketchpads and pencils. Have students snap photos or draw pictures of objects they spot on the nature walk that contain geometric shapes (e.g., circular holes in tree trunks or rectangular rocks). When you return to the classroom, have students categorize the photos and drawings according to geometric shape and post them on a bulletin board.

ART: Sketching with Shapes
YOU'LL NEED: pencils, paper, erasers
Many artists begin drawing by sketching a few geometric shapes. For example, when drawing a person, they may draw an oval head on top of a rectangular body, then add long rectangular limbs. Once the proportions are correct, they make changes (e.g., rounding the edges of the limbs) and add details. Ask students to try this technique. Provide drawing books with examples, such as *Draw 50 Animals* by Lee J. Ames (Econo-Clad, 1999).

TAKING IT FURTHER

SPOT THE SHAPES

Geometric shapes are all around us. Books are rectangles, lids are circles, and stop signs are octagons! Introduce this idea by showing students *Shapes, Shapes, Shapes* (Mulberry, 1996) or *So Many Circles, So Many Squares* (Greenwillow, 1998), both picture books by Tana Hoban, which contain photographs of familiar objects that are also geometric shapes. Then challenge students to hunt for shapes around the classroom by playing the game "I Spy." For example, one student may say, "I spy with my little eye, something in the shape of a circle." The rest of the class then scans the classroom and takes turns guessing what the object might be (e.g., "Is it the small letter 'o' on our alphabet chart?"). After playing a few rounds of the game, put the names and pictures of shapes you are studying on a large sheet of chart paper. Ask students to list the objects they found playing "I Spy" under the appropriate shape. Hang the chart in your classroom and encourage students to add to the list whenever they find new objects/shapes.

THE TANGRAM PUZZLE

A tangram is an ancient Chinese puzzle made by cutting a square of thin material (such as construction paper) into five triangles, a square, and a rhomboid. You then recombine these pieces to create many different figures, such as animals and objects. Introduce students to tangrams by reading aloud *Grandfather Tang's Story* by Ann Tompert (Dragonfly, 1997). In this tale, a grandfather uses the tangram pieces to create the animals featured in the story. Students will then be eager to try creating the creatures with tangrams. Have them follow the instructions (above, right) to make their own sets of tangram pieces. Challenge students to design their own creatures with the shapes and then to write stories about them.

HOW TO MAKE TANGRAMS

YOU NEED: 6" squares of construction paper, one per student; scissors, one pair per student

The tangram is cut from the square. Having children cut their own is a good lesson in following directions. Plus, the children are then convinced that the pieces truly go back together to make a square. The directions below show how to cut the square into seven pieces: two pairs of congruent triangles, one middle-sized triangle, one square, and one parallelogram.

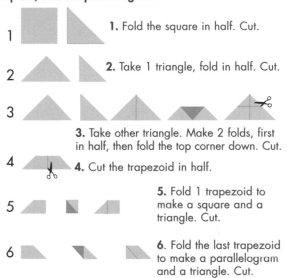

1. Fold the square in half. Cut.

2. Take 1 triangle, fold in half. Cut.

3. Take other triangle. Make 2 folds, first in half, then fold the top corner down. Cut.

4. Cut the trapezoid in half.

5. Fold 1 trapezoid to make a square and a triangle. Cut.

6. Fold the last trapezoid to make a parallelogram and a triangle. Cut.

RESOURCES

WEB SITES

http://theartcanvas.com/picasso.htm View many of Picasso's paintings.

BOOKS

The Art of Shapes: For Children and Adults by Margaret Steele and Cindy Estes (Fotofolio, 1997).

Grandfather Tang's Story: A Tale Told with Tangrams by Ann Tompert (Dragonfly, 1997).

Shapes, Shapes, Shapes by Tana Hoban (Mulberry, 1996).

So Many Circles, So Many Squares by Tana Hoban (Greenwillow, 1998).

MEETING THE STANDARDS

PRINCIPLES AND STANDARDS FOR SCHOOL MATHEMATICS

Geometry

Analyze characteristics and properties of two- and three-dimensional geometric shapes and develop mathematical arguments about geometric relationships.

MAKE CENTS OF THE

My students literally "change" the date every morning. I enlarged and cut out copies of U.S. coins, laminated them, and punched holes at the top so they could hang next to our bulletin board. During our morning meeting, I write the date on the blackboard and a designated student posts the appropriate number of coins on the board to represent it. For example, the student may represent the 18th of the month with one dime, one nickel, and three pennies. Sometimes I tell the child to use the least number of coins possible, and other times they can create the date with any combination of coins. This display does double duty, because students use it to practice making change during math time.

—*Judy Meagher*
Bozeman, MT

WHY WE LIKE THIS ACTIVITY

This stimulating morning activity engages students in problem solving while using concrete materials as models. It teaches students that there are many ways to solve problems and that many problems have more than one solution.

ADAPTING UP OR DOWN

FOR YOUNGER GRADES

After students determine the ways to make change, have them think of all of the ways to spend it by representing the date using dollars. Cut out pictures of things that are of interest to students such as toys, dolls, clothes, CDs, and foods. Paste them on cardboard, label each using a marker, and attach a price tag. Each day, have students "purchase" items (add new items regularly) and record how they spend their money in a math journal. Allow students to save their change, compute how much was left over, and apply remainders to the next day's purchase.

FOR OLDER GRADES

Have students find all the possible ways to represent the date in math terms. For example, on the 16th, the number 16 can be expressed as $0 + 16$, $20 - 4$, 2×8, $32 \div 2$, or 2^4. Have groups write as many number sentences as they can while timing the activity.

RESOURCES

WEB SITES

www.teachervision.com/lesson-plans/lesson-2637.html
This site explores dominant and recessive genes.

BOOKS

The Complete Idiot's Guide to Decoding Your Genes by Linda Tagliaferro and Mark Vincent Bloom (Macmillan, 1999).

The Cartoon Guide to Genetics by Larry Gonick and Mark Wheelis (HarperCollins, 1991).

Baa! by Cynthia Pratt Nicolson (Kids Can Press, 2001).

DATE

TAKING IT FURTHER
WORKING OUT OUTFITS

*T*each students that making combinations is part of everyday life by posing the following situation: *You only have five clean T-shirts (all different colors) and four pairs of pants (also all different colors) to wear. How many different combinations of outfits can you make? What are the possible outfits?* Prepare cutouts of shirts and pants using different colored construction paper. Ask kids to use these cutouts to find the total number of outfit combinations and draw a picture of each. Next ask them to suggest other strategies for figuring out this problem (e.g., making an organized list or a chart, or drawing a tree diagram). Distribute chart paper and have students or groups write, label, and share their strategies for solving this problem. Then alter the problem by changing the number of shirts and pants (e.g., eight shirts and five pants). Explain that multiplication can be used to find the total number of possible outfits (by multiplying the number in each set). Challenge kids by adding a selection of different colored socks. Ask: *Does adding socks to the outfit change the way we solve the problem?*

CURRICULUM CONNECTIONS
SCIENCE: Combinations of Traits

YOU'LL NEED: traits list, coins, paper plates, art supplies

Explore all the possible facial traits in an individual. Find one student who can roll his or her tongue. Tell students that the ability to roll one's tongue is a dominant trait and that most people can do it. Ask students to try rolling their tongues and then write the number of students who can as a fractional part or percent of the whole class. Then give students a chart of other facial characteristics (dominant and recessive) and have them circle each of their own traits. Using tallies, collect class data to find out how many students are dominant or recessive for each trait. Determine the percent of each dominant and recessive trait in the class. For homework, ask students to interview their family members and complete the same chart. The next day, group students and have them share their family traits. Ask students: *Which traits are most common among classmates and families? Are there recessive traits that occur in children whose parents show dominant traits? Why do you think this is so?*

When Traits Mate

Determine all the possible ways facial traits can be combined using coins to represent the dominant (heads) and recessive (tails) genes of parents. With students, use a problem-solving strategy to display all the possible gene combinations (mother's dominant/father's dominant, mother's dominant/father's recessive, mother's recessive/father's dominant, mother's recessive/father's recessive). Tell students that a recessive trait can only be passed on to an offspring when both parents have a recessive gene (in the simulation both coins must be tails). Give students a facial traits list and have them toss one coin at a time to determine the mother's gene and the father's gene. Then have students determine which trait will be passed on to the child by circling each. Allow students to use markers and other art materials to create a "paper-plate face".

FACIAL TRAITS

TRAIT	DOMINANT/RECESSIVE
HAIR TYPE	straight/curly
HAIR PATTERN	widow's peak/none
HAIR COLOR	black/brown/ blonde/red
EYELASHES	long/short
FRECKLES	yes/no
DIMPLES	yes/no
NOSE	turned up /not turned up
EAR LOBES	free/attached
EYE COLOR	dark/light

MEETING THE STANDARDS

PRINCIPLES AND STANDARDS FOR SCHOOL MATHEMATICS
Problem Solving

*S*tudents will "apply and adapt a variety of appropriate strategies to solve problems."

MEASUREMENT

WHY WE LIKE THIS ACTIVITY

*T*hese hands-on measurement activities provide practice with using measurement equipment and encourage students to hone their estimation skills.

ADAPTING UP OR DOWN

FOR YOUNGER GRADES

*D*o each measurement activity as a whole-class demonstration—one each day—and have all students make their estimates at the same time. If your class has a "buddy class," pair the older students with younger students and have them do the activities together.

TAKING IT FURTHER

*T*ry these activities for your own Measurement Olympics.

GRAM-Y AWARDS

YOU'LL NEED: a scale or triple-beam balance to measure grams, paper clips of various sizes and materials, a one-gram weight

The goal for this station is to find an object that weighs exactly one gram. The day before the Metric Olympics, show students that a paper clip is approximately one gram by weighing it on the scale. (Paper clips are of various sizes and materials, so be sure to find one that is close to one gram.) Pass around the paper clip, or a one-gram weight, so students get a feel for the weight of one gram. As a homework assignment, challenge students to bring in another object that they think weighs exactly one gram. The next day, have students place their objects on the scale to see how close they estimated.

*E*ach year, I host a Metric Measurement Olympics. I set up stations around the room with different "estimation events," such as estimating in centimeters how far students can "shotput" a cotton ball or guessing how many milliliters of water fill a fishbowl. I also put out direction cards and all the necessary materials (scales, meter sticks, etc). When students come to class, I place them in groups of four and summarize the activities at each station. Then I explain the scoring system. (Group members "compete" with the other students in their own group, and after completing each activity, the student with the closest estimation receives four points, the next closest receives three points, and so on.) Once all groups have completed each event, I award small prizes (such as rulers and tape measures) to the students who earn the most points in each group. My classes love the activities and usually talk about the Olympics for weeks!

—*Cheryl King*
Houston, TX

MEETING THE STANDARDS

PRINCIPLES AND STANDARDS FOR
SCHOOL MATHEMATICS
Measurement

*U*nderstand measurable attributes of objects and the units, systems, and processes of measurement; apply appropriate techniques, tools, and formulas to determine measurements.

OLYMPICS!

TURN UP THE VOLUME

YOU'LL NEED: a graduated cylinder (must hold at least 50 ml), several different-sized cups (each must hold at least 50 ml and should not be the same size as the graduated cylinder), water in a jug

At this station, students will try to estimate how much water equals 50 ml. Ask each student to pour water from the jug into a cup until they think they have poured exactly 50 ml. They may look at the empty graduated cylinder to help them estimate. When the entire group has water in their cups, have each student pour the contents from his or her cup into the graduated cylinder, record the volume, and then pour the water back into the jug so the next student can take his or her turn.

THE LONG AND THE SHORT OF IT

YOU'LL NEED: a ball of string or twine that does not stretch, scissors, a meter stick (placed away from the station)

With this activity, students try to estimate one meter. Have each student in the group cut a piece of string that he or she thinks is one meter long. (They may not use a meter stick or any other rulers.) After each member has cut a string, students retrieve the meter stick and measure the length of their piece of string.

"WEIGHT" A MINUTE

YOU'LL NEED: three objects (two of which—the heaviest and the lightest—are labeled with their correct weights), a scale or triple-beam balance

Present students with the three objects and ask each student to estimate the weight of the unlabeled object by comparing its weight with the known weights of the two other objects. When each member of the group has recorded an estimate, have students use the triple-beam balance to find the actual weight of the object.

"HANDY" MEASURING TOOL

YOU'LL NEED: a table or desk, rulers (placed away from the table)

With this activity, students see that they can measure objects using parts of their bodies instead of rulers. Ask students to use a ruler to measure a part of their arm or hand in centimeters and remember these lengths (e.g., my hand is 16 cm long, or my index finger is 1 cm wide). Then have each student use a body part as a tool to measure the length and width of a designated table top. Ask students to calculate the estimated area of the table top (area = L x W). When everyone in the group has written an estimation, have students use a ruler to find the actual area of the table top.

BOX PILEUP

YOU'LL NEED: boxes of various sizes, a meter stick (placed away from the station)

Without using a ruler, have each student create a tower using any of the boxes that he or she thinks will together measure 36 cm tall. When each member of the group has completed a stack, have students use a meter stick and measure the actual heights of each tower.

RESOURCES

WEB SITES

http://forum.swarthmore.edu/paths/measurement/e.measlessons.html This site has links to elementary lessons on measurement.

www.richmond.edu/~ed344/webunits/measurement/home.htm Visit the World of Measurement.

www.unc.edu/~rowlett/units/ Log on for the Dictionary of Units of Measurement.

BOOKS

How Big Is a Foot? by Rolf Myller (Econo-Clad, 1999).

How Tall, How Short, How Faraway by David A. Adler (Holiday House, 1999).

Measurement Mania: Games and Activities that Make Math Easy and Fun by Lynette Long (John Wiley & Sons, 2001).

Measuring Penny by Loreen Leedy (Henry Holt, 2000).

MATH TIPS

Time for Fun

My students have a great "time" showing off all they've learned about telling analog time. Parent volunteers paint a clock on each student's face. The kids then "read" each other's faces to practice the skills that they've learned. Finally, we parade to another class that's been studying clocks and get our faces read once more.

—*Jan Haskell*
Hampden, ME

Math-minded "Snack Shop"

For our money unit, we created a "snack shop" bulletin board. First, the children drew pictures of their favorite snacks. Then we talked about how much each snack might cost and students drew coins next to their snacks to show their monetary values. We hung the pictures on the bulletin board to create an in-class snack shop. To practice math skills, students got different amounts of imaginary money and took turns "shopping" at the snack bar. It's a fun way to bring math and money concepts to life.

—*Emma Bonilla*
New York, NY

Estimating Is a Treat

Here's an idea that keeps my students' behavior *and* estimation skills on target. Every month, I fill a clear plastic jar with a treat such as gumdrops. At the end of each day—if the entire class has behaved appropriately—students may write guesses for how many treats are in the jar. At the end of the month, I award the treats to the student with the closest estimate. Then, to help kids hone their estimation skills, we discuss the size of the next treat (e.g., jelly beans), whether their estimates should be higher or lower, and so on.

—*Pamela Flynn*
Stanford, CT

Neo Geo

If your students use geoboards to make shapes and designs, you know how tempting it is for children to pop each other with those nasty rubber bands! Try using nylon weaving loops instead. They're colorful, soft, and make much better designs.

—*Jennifer Anaya*
New Braunfels, TX

Graph It!

As part of our morning meeting, one child has the weekly job of taking attendance by asking each child a specific question, such as "What flavor of ice cream do you prefer? Chocolate, vanilla, strawberry, or other." The attendance taker records the responses in a software program on the computer. (You can use *The Graph Club* from Tom Snyder Productions.) In the program, the child chooses a graph design to represent the responses, such as a bar or pie graph, inputs the data, and prints it out. At the end of the day, we review the graph and put it in a binder to compare it to past and future graphs.

—*Florence Freda*
Cambridge, MA

Watermelon Math

To celebrate the transition from the end of summer to the first day of school, I stage a "watermelon welcome." First, I ask students to make watermelon "slices" with colored paper. They include the number of seeds they estimate a real slice will have. Then we talk about the melon's shape and objects that have similar shapes. Next I have students cut a piece of yarn to estimate how big around they think a watermelon is, and I also have them estimate its weight. Finally, I bring out a real watermelon so kids can see how close their estimates came—and we have a feast. Kids especially like eating slices to count how many seeds are in each!

—*Doris Dillon*
San Jose, CA

Fraction-Operation Chant

To tap into my students' musical intelligence, I make up songs and chants to help them remember difficult mathematical procedures. One of their favorite chants is about adding, subtracting, multiplying, and dividing fractions. I teach them one stanza at a time when I introduce each process in class.

When adding or subtracting,
Before you take your actions,
Find common denominators,
And make equivalent fractions.

To multiply/divide mixed numbers,
Make improper fractions first,
Then follow the next directions,
That we all have just rehearsed.

Before you start to multiply,
See if you can simplify,
One from top and one below,
So your answer's terms are low.

When dividing by a fraction,
Change to multiply, you see,
Then flip the *second* fraction,
And multiply like normally.

—*Laura Pye*
Montclair, NJ

Buddy Up for Math!

I teamed up with another teacher in my district for a math e-mail exchange. After we matched students by ability level, we asked each kid to create an original word problem and e-mail it to his or her pal. The following week, partners e-mailed back solutions along with new math problems. We continued the weekly exchange throughout the year. At the end of the year, students met at a party. It's a great way to practice math and communication skills—and to make new friends!

—*Lee Ann Olsen*
Mystic, CT

MATH

A Slice of Pi

I enjoy using literature and discovery activities to introduce my students to mathematical concepts. When studying circles, circumference, and pi, I read aloud to my class *Sir Cumference and the First Round Table: A Math Adventure* by Cindy Neuschwander (Charlesbridge, 1997), an imaginary tale about the origin of King Arthur's Round Table. Next, I give each pair of students a tape measure with which they measure the circumference and diameter of several circular objects they find around the classroom—coins, clocks, pencil cans, cups, etc. Then they divide each object's measured circumference by its diameter. After measuring several objects and dividing their circumferences by their diameters, students notice that no matter the size of the circle, each ratio (circumference divided by the diameter) is slightly more than three, or approximately pi. By using captivating stories and hands-on activities, difficult concepts such as pi can be fun, interactive, and memorable.

—*Tara Butler*
Minneapolis, MN

ILLUSTRATION: JOE BIAFORE

WRAPPING UP TIME

WHY WE LIKE THIS ACTIVITY

*T*his activity helps students develop an understanding of chronological time through a personalized experience. While making connections to their own lives, students learn to evaluate and sequence meaningful and significant events in time.

*E*ach fall, I "tie" together our study of time lines with our Native American unit by teaching kids about an ancient Yakima Indian Nation tradition for recording important events: time balls. These time lines are made of long lengths of string with beads tied at certain locations to represent key events. First, I ask students to brainstorm ten key events in their lives. They list such things as, "When I learned to ride a bike" or "When we moved to our new house." (I encourage kids to take their lists home to check the dates and the order of the events.) Next, they draw their time lines on a piece of paper, making sure to space out the events accurately. Then they translate their paper time lines into time balls by cutting a length of string (one foot for each year of their lives) and tying beads onto it at the proper locations of their memorable events.

Kids then sit in small groups and share their time balls with their classmates.

—*Tarry Lindquist*
Mercer Island, WA

ADAPTING UP OR DOWN

FOR YOUNGER GRADES

*T*o help students represent and sequence chronological events, create a time line of the school day. Purchase shoelaces (one for each student) and wooden beads (of at least eight different colors) from a craft store. Using the beads' colors, design a key on chart paper that coordinates with the events of the school day. (For example, use a yellow bead to represent circle time, a red bead for reading, a blue bead for math, a green bead for snack time, and so on.) At the start of the day, make a knot at one end of each shoelace and tape the other end to each student's desk. After each activity, refer to the key and have students string the correct bead. At the end of the day, have small groups or partners retell one another the significant events in sequence. Send each student home with a copy of the key and ask parents and caregivers to listen to the retelling of a very eventful day!

FOR OLDER GRADES

*H*ave students visit younger students to share their personal time balls. After students have shared, ask them to trade time balls and attempt to retell one another's memorable events. Then use the time balls to launch writing workshops for personal narratives or memoirs.

LINES

TAKING IT FURTHER

MAKE IT MEMORABLE

*H*ave students personalize their time balls by making their own beads using *Crayola Model Magic Modeling Compound*. Give kids white compound and have them decorate dry beads with paint. Or give them a variety of compounds and have them blend the colors together. Encourage kids to mold the compound into shapes (cubed, round, oval, etc.) that symbolize each of their memorable events. Use toothpicks and engrave the dates of the memorable events on the time balls. Then have kids use skewers to pierce each ball of clay and allow the beads to air-dry.

A YEARLONG PROJECT

*M*ark the passage of each week by documenting important classroom events and creating a yearlong time line. Secure string along the walls of the classroom. Label index cards with specific dates and attach them to the string using clothespins. (For example, Week 1: September 8-12). Use a ruler to measure even distances between each week. On the first day of school, take a photo of your class and clip it to the time line. Wrap up the week by discussing events and choosing a student to write a summary. Throughout the year, update the time line each week by attaching student summaries and illustrations. Include important occurrences such as trips, visitors, assemblies, and newsworthy current events.

CURRICULUM CONNECTIONS

SCIENCE: Timely Inventions
YOU'LL NEED: butcher paper and art materials
Incorporate time lines into your science curriculum by having your class create an "Invention Time Line." Narrow the study to a specific time period such as the Industrial Revolution or focus on a topic, such as household products or modes of transportation. For example, your class could create a "Weather Inventions Time Line" that includes such things as the anemometer, barometer, weather vane, thermometer, weather balloon, and so on. Before putting the time line together, have students do research to learn more about the significant inventions for your topic. Make a list of these significant inventions and ask each student to choose one they would like to learn more about. Have students collect reference materials and write a short report on the invention they chose. Make sure they include who the inventor was, what the invention does, how it is used, when and where it was invented, why it is an important tool, and what its impact has been on society. After students complete their reports, have the class put the inventions into chronological order and create a time line on butcher paper. As an extension, ask students to create models of the inventions they researched using a variety of art materials. Set up an "Invention Convention" in the gym or hallway where students can display their models and reports along the time line. Invite other classes to walk along the "Invention Time Line" and experience scientific history in the "re-making!"

RESOURCES

BOOKS

100 Inventions That Shaped World History by Bill Yenne (Bluewood Books, 1993).

Eyewitness: Invention by Lionel Bender (DK, 2000).

WEB SITES

www.invent.org/book/ The National Inventors Hall of Fame.

www.crayola.com Modeling compound available here.

MEETING THE STANDARDS

NATIONAL COUNCIL FOR THE SOCIAL STUDIES
Time, Continuity, and Change
Identify key concepts such as chronology, causality, and change. Read and construct simple time lines.

GREETING CARD

A+
activities

I've found a great way to tie in our economics and business unit with any holiday! Groups of four students create a greeting card from a pre-specified quantity of plain paper, crepe paper, and pipe cleaners (e.g., 1 sheet of plain paper, 2 sheets of crepe paper, and 3 pipe cleaners). And they time how long it takes them. Kids then calculate the time and supplies they would need to create 100 of the same cards. As a class, we discuss how assembly lines could speed things up and cut costs. I ask kids to imagine the journey these cards would take from production to purchase by customers. My students say they'll never look at a store-bought card the same way again.

—Karen Myers
New York, NY

WHY WE LIKE THIS ACTIVITY

Through a realistic problem-solving situation, this productive activity demonstrates two methods of manufacturing goods. It allows kids to interact independently as well as in groups to assemble a product and then evaluate the process.

ADAPTING UP OR DOWN

FOR YOUNGER GRADES

Have students investigate the idea that many hands make light work. Keep track of the number of minutes it takes each child to make his or her own card by listing names and times on the board. Ask the class to share their cards and then choose one card that groups of kids will make together. Separate students into groups of four and have kids choose a part of the card to complete. Time the number of minutes it takes the class to work cooperatively to make approximately 20 cards. Read the poem "Helping" by Shel Silverstein and have students discuss situations when they like to work alone and when they need help from others.

FOR OLDER GRADES

Use the card-making activity to demonstrate the difference between a cottage industry and the mass production of goods using assembly lines. Have each student make his or her own card and then a mass-produced card as a member of an assembly line. Discuss the advantages and disadvantages by asking students the following questions: *Which method produced a better card? Which method did you prefer/not prefer? What changes would you make to produce even more cards (speed up the process)? What did you like most/least about your task?*

MEETING THE STANDARDS

CURRICULUM STANDARDS FOR SOCIAL STUDIES
Production, Distribution, and Consumption
Give examples of the various institutions that make up economic systems and how we depend upon workers with specialized jobs.

BUSINESS

TAKING IT FURTHER

ON SALE!

*A*fter students make mass-produced cards, have them compile a list of materials they used. Then identify the exact amount of each item that was needed. (For example, 25 sheets of plain paper, 50 sheets of crepe paper, and 75 pipe cleaners). Provide groups with a variety of advertisements from office, craft, and educational supply stores. Tell students to "shop" for the best deals on materials needed to create another set of holiday cards and find a total. Then figure out how much it costs to make one card and how much to charge to make a profit.

RESOURCES

WEB SITES

www.learn2.com/06/0697/0697.asp
www.papershops.com/papershops/papermaking/makepaper.html
Log on to these sites to learn more about making recycled paper.

BOOKS

Where the Sidewalk Ends: The Poems and Drawings of Shel Silverstein by Shel Silverstein (HarperCollins, 1974).

CURRICULUM CONNECTIONS

ART: From Plant to Pulp to Paper
YOU'LL NEED: 2-4 newspapers, a food processor, white glue, a sink full of water, insect screens, several pieces of wool, a clothesline or drying rack, an electric iron

The card-making activity engages students in the process of making a product from start to finish using two different types of paper. Take students even further back through the process by having them make their own paper! Explain that making paper is an ancient tradition. The Egyptians made paper from the plant papyrus, the Chinese from rice, and the Europeans from animal skins! Today most paper is made from cellulose found in plant fibers (usually from trees). Because of the threat to the environment, many people recycle paper. Recycled paper is easy to make, saves trees, and uses little electricity.

Begin by creating a concept web showing different kinds of paper and their uses. Then provide students with examples of paper bags, tissue paper, toilet paper, wrapping papers, parchment, and newspaper. Let them examine each to notice similarities and differences.

Divide your students into teams of five with each member of the team assigned one of the following tasks: Tear, Grind, Glue, Strain, and Dry. The Tear person rips pieces of newspaper into 1-inch squares (about a cup of these is needed to make each piece of recycled paper). The Grinder assists the teacher in mixing the newspaper and water in the food processor (filled about $1/2$ way) for about 3 minutes to form a gray blob. The Glue person adds 2 to 3 tablespoons of glue to sink water (about $3/4$ full) and then mixes in the pulp. The Strainers submerge the insect screen to the bottom of the sink and raise it slowly (counting to 20) to lift the pulp out of the water (moving their hands from side to side). The Dryers lay the paper out on wool squares and then hang it up on the clothesline to dry. Teams then use rolling pins to flatten the dry paper as the teacher presses it using an electric iron.

For paper variety, have each Tear person add thread, flowers, feathers, or leaves. During the grinding stage, have students add food coloring or scented oils. Then try substituting different types of adhesives or cornstarch during the glue stage and have students decide which works the best.

PIECES OF OUR STATE

A+ activities

WHY WE LIKE THIS ACTIVITY

*T*his activity is a colorful, collaborative way to learn about one's state while meeting state and national social studies standards. And when you're done, you have a great bulletin board!

ADAPTING UP OR DOWN

FOR YOUNGER GRADES

*M*ake a large bulletin-board outline of your state. Discuss its shape and then distribute state outline maps to each student. Gather resources and materials about your state, and bookmark appropriate Web sites (see Resources, opposite). Have each student find one important fact about your state. Georgia, for example, is known for its peaches. Let students write and/or illustrate the facts on their individual outline maps and then share with the class.

With students, find the approximate location of your town or city on the large outline map and write its name next to a dot indicating its location. Next locate and mark the capital of your state, important cities, and other information such as significant rivers, mountains, and landmarks. Discuss these various aspects as you mark them on the map.

Cut the state outline into arbitrary puzzle pieces or cut into pieces representing regions of your state, laminate the puzzle pieces, and use as a floor map for further reinforcement and fun.

FOR OLDER GRADES

*W*hen your students are studying the United States or regions of our country, assign each student a state(s) or ask them to team up to research a region. They can also do this activity with other countries and continents.

*n*o matter the size of the state, each one has special features. My students learn about the various areas of our state by creating a state puzzle. I draw a bulletin-board-sized outline map of Montana on butcher paper and divide it into puzzle pieces. I then assign one piece to each student and ask them to mark the approximate locations of their pieces on their own 8 1/2" x 11" maps of the state. Next, we cut the puzzle apart. Students research their particular area, record notes and facts on the backs of their puzzle pieces, and draw pictures depicting the areas' towns, landmarks, and local industries on the fronts. Then they share the pictures and information about their sections and glue the puzzle back together to create a colorful bulletin board. Now, learning about our state doesn't leave my students puzzled!

—*Judy Meagher*
Bozeman, MT

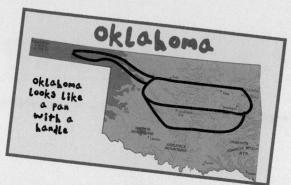

oklahoma

oklahoma looks like a pan with a handle

TAKING IT FURTHER

*H*ave students plan a one-week trip through a region of your state or from one part of your state to another. Bring in travel guides, brochures, and state maps as references. Bookmark appropriate Web sites (see Resources, below). Give students a reproducible map of your state and a budget. Then instruct them to map out a driving route to get from point A to point B and mark the approximate locations and names of places to stay, special landmarks to visit, and things to do. Encourage students to share their trips with the class and then take them home to share with their parents. Who knows? Maybe some of these virtual trips will become realities!

RESOURCES

WEB SITES
For students
www.50states.com Log on to this site to find out about each state's flag and symbols, maps, constitution, representatives, and more!

www.ipl.org/youth/stateknow/ This site includes a wealth of information about each state—size and population, date it entered the Union, symbols, sports teams, and other fascinating facts.

BOOKS
For teachers
Ready-to-Go Super Book of Outline Maps (Scholastic, 2000).

Ready-to-Use Outline Maps of U.S. States and Regions (Dover, 1994).

Know the World! by David Green (Tarquin, 1993).

CURRICULUM CONNECTIONS

SCIENCE/SOCIAL STUDIES/MATH:
Putting All the Pieces Together
YOU'LL NEED: Several bulletin-board-sized state outline maps (one for each small group cut into pieces according to the various regions of the state), state reference books including atlases, crayons, markers, glue, and 5" x 7" index cards (one per student).

Assign groups to research different aspects of your state, such as plants and animals, industry and agriculture, landforms, population, and elevation. Each person in the group can take a different region or puzzle piece and research the group's topic. Have students draw symbols or pictures on their map pieces and write captions about their facts on large index cards.

Then have each group place the pieces of their puzzle together, secure the pieces with tape or staples, draw leaders, and attach index cards that tell about each region. For example, *Industry and Agriculture in Oklahoma's Red Carpet Country—cattle ranching and wheat farming.*

Display the groups' maps on bulletin boards or the wall. Or staple the various maps on a bulletin board in layers so students can lift them and see all the aspects of an area/region. By looking at state maps that highlight particular features, students will be able to make important connections. For example, "The rich, fertile soil of the plains region of Kansas is why so much corn is grown there," "New Orleans is a historic city—that's why tourism is a thriving industry in this region of Louisiana," and so on.

MEETING THE STANDARDS

CURRICULUM STANDARDS FOR SOCIAL STUDIES
People, Places, and Environments
*E*xamine the interaction of human beings and their physical environment, the use of land, building of cities, and ecosystem changes in selected locales and regions. Consider existing uses of resources and land in home, school, community, the region, and beyond.

A+ Activities

WHY WE LIKE THIS ACTIVITY

This is a wonderful way to bring children from various cultures together. Students will learn that in spite of differences in such things as language, food, and styles of dress, we are all more alike than different. With the nations of the world becoming more and more closely linked, cultural understandings and appreciation are increasingly important.

I found a way to integrate multiculturalism throughout my curriculum. At the beginning of the year I guide each student in a search for an international pen pal. I coordinate the search so my students find pen pals from all over the world. (See Resources, opposite, for information about finding pen pals for students.) Then I set up a bulletin board with a world map, and students mark their pen pals' locations with names and colored push pins. I allot 30 minutes every other week for students to write to their pen pals. In their letters, students ask their pen pals questions about the countries in which they live, school and education, food, clothes, recreation, books, holidays and celebrations, TV shows, and so on. Whenever students receive a reply from their pen pals, they share with the class what they have learned. Besides the great friendships that develop and the real-world writing practice this activity brings about, my students learn a lot about different countries around the world and the lives of people who live there.

—*Sara Williams*
New York, NY

ADAPTING UP OR DOWN

FOR YOUNGER GRADES

Have the whole class correspond with a few classes around the world (rather than finding a pen pal for each student). As your students dictate their messages to you, type them out, review with the class, and e-mail or send.

FOR OLDER GRADES

Suggest that students send their pen pals photos, cassettes, and drawings, and have them request that their pen pals send them similar artifacts. Have each student keep a folder of his or her pen pal's correspondence and materials.

CONNECTIONS

TAKING IT FURTHER

INTERNATIONAL DAYS

Explain to students that each one of them is going to lead the class in celebrating one of his or her pen pal's favorite holidays.

Schedule students' celebrations after they have had enough time to develop relationships with their pen pals and gathered enough information about the origins and meanings of the holidays. Have students include specifics about how the holidays are celebrated—e.g., special clothes or costumes, foods, and activities. Encourage students to do further research on their celebrations in reference books and on the Internet.

RESOURCES

WEB SITES

www.ks-connection.org/ Kids' Space Connection is a great site for kids who want international e-mail pen pals.

www.world-pen-pals.com/ Visit the World Pen Pals site to find an international pen pal to exchange letters with. For more information, call (845) 246-7828 or write to P.O. Box 337, Saugerties, NY 12477.

BOOKS

Wake Up World! A Day in the Life of Children Around the World by Beatrice Hollyer (Henry Holt, 1999).

Children from Australia to Zimbabwe: A Photographic Journey Around the World by Maya Ajmera and Anna Rhesa Versola (Charlesbridge, 1997).

CURRICULUM CONNECTIONS

MATH: Time Zones

YOU'LL NEED: atlas, Internet connection

Review that as the Earth rotates, it is day in the part of the world facing the Sun, and night in the part of the world in shadow. Explain that the Earth is divided into 24 standard time zones. Have students use a world atlas or log on to www.timeanddate.com to see all the different time zones. Then ask students: *If it is 1 pm (in your town or city) what time is it in your pen pal's town or city?* Distribute square pieces of paper with clock faces without hands. Have students draw the appropriate time by adding hands to the clock face. Then let students show their clock's time, explain how they determined it, and relate to the class what activities their pen pal might be engaged in at that time. Display the clocks on the world map bulletin board next to each pen pal's name.

LANGUAGE ARTS: How Do You Say?

YOU'LL NEED: foreign language dictionaries, foreign language conversational guide books

Have students learn simple conversational words and phrases in their pen pal's language, such as *hello, good-bye, How are you?, Where is the. . . ?* and so on. Have children practice writing and saying some of these words and phrases. You may wish to make charts comparing ways pen pals say "Hello" or suggest that students try out some of the words they've learned on their pen pals in their next letter.

MEETING THE STANDARDS

CURRICULUM STANDARDS FOR SOCIAL STUDIES
Culture

Describe ways in which language, stories, folktales, music, and artistic creations serve as expressions of culture and influence behavior of people living in a particular culture.

Global Connections

Explore ways that language, art, music, belief systems, and other cultural elements may facilitate global understanding or lead to misunderstanding.

Focus on Geography

I start each geography class with a quick round of "F.O.G."—Focus On Geography! As the members of each of four teams I've designated (north, south, east, and west) trickle in from other classes, I start a timer at two minutes, and team members work to complete as many answers from the day's F.O.G. activity as possible before the timer goes off. Activities are varied, such as "list as many landlocked African countries as you can" or "name all the capitals of countries in Central America." We then check the answers by exchanging papers. This quick activity not only gets kids excited about geography, it's also a great transition to start class and get students in the mood to learn.

—*Linda Norman*
Ayer, MA

Postcards from America

I kick off Geography Awareness Week each November with an activity that teaches about the 50 states and gives my second-graders authentic writing practice. I use an overhead projector to copy a U.S. map onto poster board. Then I have students write to friends and relatives across the country asking them to send postcards picturing something significant about their state—such as a famous landmark or a distinguishing physical feature. As postcards hit our mailbox, we hang them in the appropriate places on the map.

—*Linda Valentino*
Slate Hill, NY

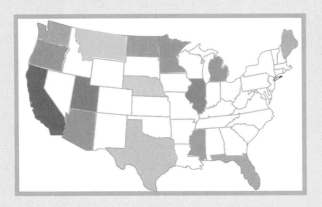

PUZZLING STATES

I make a plastic place mat showing the map of the 50 states for each of my students to keep on his or her desk. Each day, I challenge students to name as many states as they can and find their locations. With a roomful of other map puzzles, plus a playful attitude, they learn all the states' names and locations in just a few weeks!

— *Deborah Fente,*
Torrance, CA

Which Way?

In my first-grade classroom I put up signs on the wall labeling the four main directions: north, south, east, and west. Using a globe, I show children these four cardinal directions as well as the North Pole and South Pole. Then I place my finger on the equator and start moving it toward the North Pole. After asking my students what direction I am going, I point to the north side of the classroom and say, "This way to the North Pole." I explain that if they are facing north, the west will always be on their left, the east on their right and the south behind them. Then I reinforce students' understanding of directions with activities that involve movement. I ask them to line up on the north side of the room, pass their papers to the west, exit by the south door, meet at the reading table on the east side of the room, and so on.

—*Margaret Mooney*
Minneapolis, MN

GEOGRAPHY!

Create a Puzzle Map!

Try this for Geography Awareness Week. Last year my fifth-graders made a fact-packed puzzle map of the United States. To begin, I assigned different states to groups of students. Using the overhead, kids projected a U.S. map onto poster board, traced the outlines of their states, and cut them out. On the cutouts, they wrote information, such as the state's nickname, population, climate characteristics, motto, and flower. (For smaller states, they created separate "information cards.") Kids added illustrations of state flags and pinpointed state capitals with gold stars. Finally, they pieced the map together on the wall. It's a great cooperative project!

—Melissa Hoover
Concord Township, OH

PEELINGS

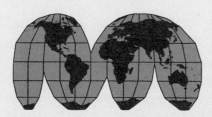

After studying the difference between maps and globes I have my students do the following activity to show how maps cause distortion. I have students draw a picture around the outside of an orange peel. Next, I have them carefully peel the orange all in one piece, and then flatten the peel on the table. As students realize their drawing has become twisted or distorted I explain that this is what happens when maps of the whole Earth are made.

—Joan Mason
San Jose, CA

Latitude & Longitude Acrostics

After studying latitude and longitude I demonstrate how to find a global "address." I start by having students locate the approximate latitude and longitude of our city and other cities such as Amsterdam, Moscow, Santiago, and Honolulu. Then I ask my students to pinpoint the following series of coordinates: 40° N, 3° W; 38° N, 23° E; 40° N, 75° W; 33° S, 151° E. I have them use a globe or atlas to find the major cities nearest each point and challenge them to take the first letter from each city and see what word it spells. Students then challenge one another by choosing sets of coordinates that make a variety of acrostics.

—Mary Matthews
Ann Arbor, MH

Worldly People

I photocopy outline maps of countries around the world and distribute them to students. I have them cut out the countries they want to use and arrange them so as to make a person. On the back of each outline map, students write the name of the country and important national facts. I challenge students to name their person and then I hang their work from the ceiling for all to enjoy.

—Angela Bordeaux
Annapolis, MD

UNRAVEL THE

BIOGRAPHY BOARD AND DEBATE PHOTOS: JUDI SLEPYAN

PEEK-THROUGH BIOGRAPHY BOARDS

My students were tired of doing the "same old, same old" oral reports, so I decided to spice things up for Women's History Month (March). After students researched influential women of the past, I asked them to write their reports in the first person (e.g., "I am Amelia Earhart"). I then asked them to cut a large round hole (big enough to fit their heads through) near the top of a piece of poster board. They then drew a picture of their famous woman on the poster board and cut two holes through it for their hands. Students "donned" their poster boards to do their reports. What a great way to relive history!

—*Tarry Lindquist*
Mercer Island, WA

TELLING TOTEMS

When studying the Tlingit Native Americans of the Pacific Northwest we discuss how they carved totem poles into animals that represented the guardian spirits of their clan, or family. I then have my students create their own totem poles from wrapping paper rolls or oatmeal containers. Each totem pole consists of containers attached end to end and then mounted on a sturdy piece of cardboard as a base. Students glue pictures of themselves and their families (hand drawn or snapshots) and attach them to one side of the totem pole. On colored index cards students write a story explaining their family's history and attach the cards to the pole's opposite side. I then have students think about an animal that could symbolize their family. They draw the face of the animal and place this picture on top of the totem pole. When students have finished making their totem poles they take turns explaining the symbolism of their chosen animal and relate their family history. Kids have a lot of fun and really treasure their totem poles.

—*Antoinette Bianco*
Brooklyn, NY

TRICKS OF THE TRADE

I bring career awareness to our study of Thanksgiving by having kids take a look at colonial-era trades. First, I divide students into groups and assign each group a different master trade: whitesmith (works with tin), apothecary (pharmacist), cooper (makes barrels), silversmith (repairs or makes things with silver), schoolmaster (a teacher), joiner (makes cabinets and furniture), blacksmith (works with iron), and cobbler (makes shoes). Then, kids research the trade and create construction-paper symbols for each, such as lanterns and candlesticks to symbolize a whitesmith. In the end, we turn the symbols into a trademark display.

—*Lara D. Davis*
Columbia, MS

Immigration Quilts

Our Immigration Quilt Project is a rewarding activity that brings history into the classroom in a way that's truly personal. Each child chooses a relative who has immigrated to the United States. They do extensive interviews with family members, or the person who immigrated, to learn about that person and his or her journey. Students then each draw nine sketches that illustrate various aspects of their relatives' lives in their former countries, their actual journeys to America, and their families. From these sketches, students create nine squares made of colorful fabric, and then paste them onto large pieces of sturdy material such as denim or corduroy. Some students have even personalized the quilts with actual pieces of material that belonged to their relatives. We then invite family and friends to hear the stories behind the quilts. I enjoy this project so much that I even made a quilt about my grandmother which now decorates her wall.

—*Amy Gotliffe*
San Francisco, CA

MYSTERY OF HISTORY

Greetings from the Mayflower

After reading several books about the Mayflower, my students pretend they are passengers on this historic ship. They begin by writing detailed journal entries as though they were on the journey and give the paper an

old, authentic look by smearing brown chalk along the edges. Then they take photographs of each other with digital cameras, print them out, stick their faces on the "bodies" of their journal entries, and add decorative period hats. These personal touches really encourage my students to get into the roles of the seafaring pioneers aboard the Mayflower.

—*Christine M. Griffin*
Stratford, CT

ROADSIDE REMEMBRANCES

My fourth-grade class studies historic monuments, such as the Statue of Liberty, Mount Rushmore, the Liberty Bell, Plymouth Rock, and the St. Louis Gateway Arch. We discuss the monuments themselves and their symbolism. Then we read inscriptions from the monuments and talk about what information they contain. After we discuss several markers, I have students pick a person, place, or event in our own city to commemorate with a monument. First they must do research to pick a worthy subject and then decide on an appropriate marker to construct, such as a clay statue of a historic figure. Then they write an inscription that answers the five W's about the person, place, or thing that is being memorialized. We set these monuments up throughout the school so other students can learn more about our city.

—*Susan Shay*
St. Louis, MO

CLASS CONGRESS

Teaching third-graders about passing bills in Congress can be fun when they act out the process. I divide the class into the House of Representatives and the Senate, with more students in the House because of the actual proportion in Congress. Students bring bills to their respective "floors" or groups to try and get them passed (e.g., "We should be able to eat in the room on Fridays"). As in Congress, the bills have to get passed by both branches and then be passed along to the President (teacher) to sign or reject. In addition to learning about passing laws in Congress, my students learn to work together and make decisions.

—*Tod Petit*
Mansfield, OH

Create a Debate

Whenever elections are approaching, my students enjoy debating the issues—just like the candidates do! We begin by watching news programs on television to find hot topics, such as endangered species and deforestation. They then pick a topic, do a random drawing to determine which students will represent each side, research the pros and cons of the issue, and stage a formal debate. This activity helps students understand the issues in the upcoming elections and learn the importance of being informed voters.

—*Tarry Lindquist*
Mercer Island, WA

WHY WE LIKE THIS ACTIVITY

*T*his bulletin board can easily be changed as often as you like to match the current environment. It brings a bit of nature into the classroom and shows students how their activities are influenced by the changing seasons.

*T*o bring the great outdoors into my classroom, I've made a 3-D tree on my wall from rolls of brown paper. Each season, I decorate it with photos of my students and seasonal motifs. In the fall, I put autumn leaves and apples on it; in the winter, I line each branch with white cotton "snow;" and in spring, I decorate it with bright blossoms and birds' nests. Students really enjoy seeing the changes the tree takes each season.

—Doris Dillon
San Jose, CA

ADAPTING UP OR DOWN

FOR YOUNGER GRADES

A few days before you change the tree's "decor," (e.g., from fall leaves to bare branches), take students on a walk outside to observe the changes in the trees and surrounding environment. When you return to the classroom, ask them what they think should be added or taken away from the bulletin board tree to make it look like the outside environment. After you change the features to match the season, ask students to draw pictures of seasonal activities. For example, when you add autumn leaves to the branches, students can draw pictures of themselves carving pumpkins, raking leaves, playing football, and so on. Post these pictures around the tree to demonstrate seasonal activities.

FOR OLDER GRADES

*I*n addition to posting students' photographs on the tree (on cutouts of apples, fall leaves, snowflakes, blossoms, etc.), ask students to write about the change in seasons and post their writing on similar seasonal cutouts. You may wish to ask students to write in a different style each season, such as haiku in fall, limericks in spring, and so on.

MEETING THE STANDARDS

NATIONAL SCIENCE EDUCATION STANDARDS

Life Science—Characteristics of Organisms
*T*he behavior of an individual organism is influenced by internal cues (such as hunger) and by external cues (such as changes in the environment).

Life Science—Life Cycles of Organisms
*P*lants and animals have life cycles that include being born, developing into adults, reproducing, and eventually dying.

TAKING IT FURTHER

THE CYCLES OF LIFE

The changes the tree makes throughout the seasons provide a perfect focal point for learning about other cyclic processes in nature. When the tree's leaves fall, discuss decomposition and how decaying leaves add nutrients to the soil. On a rainy or snowy day, or during the rainy months in the spring, discuss the water cycle. Place signs on and around the tree that label how water is recycled through evaporation, rain, leaves giving off water vapor (transpiration), absorption through plant roots, filtering through soil, and surface runoff. On a sunny day, highlight the photosynthetic process and how photosynthesis gives plants nutrients they need. And when insects emerge in the spring, discuss the food chain, explaining how a tree is a food source for an insect, which may be hunted by a bird, which may be hunted by another animal, etc.

RESOURCES

WEB SITES

www.worldbook.com/fun/seasons/html/seasons.htm
Learn about what causes seasons and more.

www.brainpop.com
Children will enjoy viewing short science movies, including ones on seasons and autumn leaves.

BOOKS

An Apple Tree Through the Year by Claudia Schnieper (Carolrhoda, 1987).

Crafts for All Seasons by Kathy Ross (Millbrook, 2000).

The Reasons for Seasons by Gail Gibbons (Holiday House, 1995).

The Seasons of Arnold's Apple Tree by Gail Gibbons (Harcourt Brace, 1988).

Sky Tree: Seeing Science Through Art by Thomas Locker (HarperCollins, 1995).

CURRICULUM CONNECTIONS

SOCIAL STUDIES: We Need Trees
YOU'LL NEED: old magazines, scissors, chart paper, markers
Trees provide many products and foods that we use every day, such as paper, cardboard, wood, apples, and cherries. Read a book that highlights some of the products and foods that come from trees, such as *The Giving Tree* by Shel Silverstein (HarperCollins, 1986) or *Be a Friend to Trees* by Patricia Lauber (HarperCollins, 1994). Ask students to name products and foods that come from trees, and list their responses on chart paper. Post the list and ask students to continue to add to it. Then ask students to bring in small examples or magazine clippings of products or foods that come from trees. They can post them on the parts of the tree from which the products come. For example, a picture of an orange would be posted hanging from the branches, while a wooden toy boat would be posted on the trunk of the tree.

ART: Painting and Printing
YOU'LL NEED: Apples, bark, leaves, twigs, pine needles, pinecones, seeds, acorns, crayons, chalk, paint, paper
Take students on a nature walk to collect fallen leaves, twigs, pieces of bark, acorns, and so on. (Or gather the materials ahead of time and bring them to class.) Display all the findings and ask students to think about how they can use them to create a work of art. Then try some of the following ideas: ✔Make rubbings by placing a piece of paper over a leaf (or piece of bark) and rubbing crayons or chalk over the paper. ✔Use twigs or pine needles as paintbrushes. ✔Make prints by dipping pinecones, apple pieces, pussy willows, or leaves in paint and stamping them on a piece of paper. ✔Paint tiny faces on acorns. ✔Glue various tree seeds in designs on paper. For detailed instructions on making "natural" art supplies, such as inks, paints, and printing materials, read *Berry Smudges and Leaf Prints* by Ellen B. Senisi (Dutton, 2001).

BLOOMING BUDS

A+ Activities

WHY WE LIKE THIS ACTIVITY

*T*his is an integrative, seasonal activity. Not only are students planting flower bulbs (science), measuring the heights of the shoots (math), drawing pictures of the flowers (art), and predicting what they will look like the next day (critical thinking skills), but they are also taking the flowers to local hospitals (community service)!

*O*n the first day of spring last year, my students' prediction and graphing skills began to blossom. We planted amaryllis and narcissus bulbs in pots. Each day children recorded the heights of the growing plants on line graphs. Students also drew pictures to predict what the plants would look like the next day and how tall they'd be. Once the flowers were in full bloom, we shared their beauty by donating them to a local children's hospital.

—*Carole Keister*
McClellandtown, PA

ADAPTING UP OR DOWN

FOR YOUNGER GRADES

*P*lant a bulb as a whole-class project. Two or three times a week during your morning meeting, ask a different student to water and measure the plant. Guide that student as he or she places a piece of string at the base of the plant and measures vertically to the height of its tallest part. Then have the child cut the string to that length. Tape the strings in chronological order on a line graph. Ask students to predict the height of the plant before placing the new string on the graph. Also, ask them to predict when the flower will bloom. Ask other questions, such as: *Do you think the plant will be taller or shorter than yesterday? How much taller or shorter do you think it will be?*

FOR OLDER GRADES

*P*lace students in groups of three or four. Have each group plant a bulb and take care of it. After the plants start to grow, groups can measure the heights of their plants two or three times a week and chart the heights on their own graphs. Once a week, ask each group for the current height of its plant. Record the heights on the chalkboard and ask students to calculate the average height of the plants.

MEETING THE STANDARDS

NATIONAL SCIENCE EDUCATION STANDARDS
Life Science—The Characteristics of Organisms

*O*rganisms have basic needs. For example, animals need air, water, and food; plants require air, water, nutrients, and light. Organisms can survive only in environments in which their needs can be met.

TAKING IT FURTHER

CONDUCTING A CONTROLLED EXPERIMENT

*R*eview the lesson on growing bulbs by asking students what the bulb needs in order to grow. Ask them to choose one factor or variable (such as sunlight, water, or soil) and to conduct an experiment to see how changing this factor affects the plant's growth. Ask students to follow the scientific method and to use the following procedure: Have them plant two bulbs. One bulb they will use as the control, treating it "normally," giving it an appropriate amount of water and sunlight. With the other bulb, they will change only one variable to see the effect the change has on the plant. One group, for example, may test what happens when a plant is placed under a plant light 24 hours a day, while another group may put its plant in a closet so it receives no light at all. Or one group will give its plant only bottled water while another gives its plant only water from a local creek. Ask students to keep a detailed log about what they do with both bulbs and record the results. Then have them draw a conclusion as to how changing that one factor affected the growth of the plant. Let students make posters that display their results.

RESOURCES

WEB SITES

www.kidsgardening.com
Log on to this site from the National Gardening Association for classroom ideas, grants, and resources about gardening with children.

www.urbanext.uiuc.edu/bulbs/index.html
Learn about how to select, plant, and care for flower bulbs.

BOOKS

Eyewitness Explorers: Flowers by David Burnie (DK Publishing, 1997).

How a Plant Grows by Bobbie Kalman (Crabtree, 1996).

The Magic School Bus Plants Seeds: A Book About How Living Things Grow by Joanna Cole (Scholastic, 1995).

Plants Feed on Sunlight: And Other Facts About Things That Grow by Helen Taylor (Copper Beech, 1998).

What Makes a Flower Grow? by Susan Mayes (Usborne, 1989).

CURRICULUM CONNECTIONS

WRITING: Point-of-view Journal
YOU'LL NEED: pencils and paper
As an exercise in "point-of-view" writing, ask students to write journal entries as if they were a bulb, seed, or flower. Students may wish to write from the perspective of a bulb/seed/flower that is begging for more light, one that is receiving too much water and is jealous of others that are getting less water, or one that is ready to show the world its colors. Have students draw a picture to accompany the journal entry.

DRAMA/DANCE: Acting Out the Stages
YOU'LL NEED: music tapes and player (optional)
Ask students to act out the stages a plant progresses through as it grows. They may start in a tight ball shape as if they were a seed, and then slowly reach toward the sky. Or use *Children's Book of Yoga: Games & Exercises Mimic Plants & Animals & Objects* by Thia Luby (Clear Light, 1998) for examples of yoga positions that represent a flower's growth. This book shows photographs of children demonstrating yoga poses, along with pictures of the plants, animals, and objects that inspired the positions, such as tulips opening or trees standing balanced and tall.

A+ Activities

CLASSIFICATION

WHY WE LIKE THIS ACTIVITY

*T*his activity is a delicious, fun way to have kids learn a scientific procedure and develop decision-making skills. You may wish to have kids classify other items such as beans, beads, and shells.

ADAPTING UP OR DOWN

FOR YOUNGER GRADES

*U*sing masking tape, map out a large "candy trail" (classification key) on the gymnasium floor or playground that your class can "walk" through to categorize candy (or other items). Label the start of the trail "All Candies" and make arrows that point in opposite directions. Write out the classification criteria on index cards and place them in squares along the trail. Have kids pick a candy and walk to the square that describes it. Continue to have kids read the criteria in each successive square and decide which way to move. As they travel along the trail, point out the similarities and differences among the items. Continue to have students make distinctions by following the trail, deciding which direction to move, and walking to the next square. Eventually, each student will classify his or her candy from the most general to the most specific attribute and reach a final position on the trail.

*M*y sixth-grade science students study plant and animal classification in late October. I take advantage of the season by assigning kids to make a classification (or dichotomous) key for their Halloween candy. Each student chooses 25 different pieces of candy. They then separate the candy into two categories. For example, the first two groups may be "chocolate" and "not chocolate," or "red on the wrapper" and "no red on the wrapper." They continue to break down each group by using only one criterion until there is just one candy item in each category. The kids really enjoy choosing the categories, and it's a great way to make their candy last a little longer!

—Marilyn M. Nipper
Millbrook, AL

FOR OLDER GRADES

*H*ave each student make a classification key of his or her own. Then have kids trade keys with a partner and classify the candy using different criteria. Encourage students to use concept-mapping software such as *Inspiration* to create a dynamic key that distinguishes each criterion using various colors, shapes, and patterns.

MEETING THE STANDARDS

NATIONAL SCIENCE EDUCATION STANDARDS
Understandings About Science as Inquiry
*T*ypes of investigations include describing objects, events, and organisms; classifying them; and doing a fair test (experimenting).

TAKING IT FURTHER

TAKE A LOOK AT LEAVES

Give students a chance to act like botanists and identify regional leaves and trees. Using brown bags, let them collect leaves from the school playground or a nearby park. (A day prior, use reference materials or the Internet to show students pictures of poison ivy, poison oak, poison sumac, and other problem plants in your area. Make sure students know how to identify and avoid them.) In the classroom, have students group the leaves according to specific characteristics, such as color, size, shape, texture, lobes, or vein pattern. Ask them to measure the length and width of each leaf and write a description. Then have kids identify the scientific name of the plant from which each leaf comes using reference materials (see Resources). Provide examples, such as "Sassafras Leaves *(Sassafras albidum)*. These leaves are about 5″ long, bright green, aromatic, and may have 3, 2, or no lobes." Have students press the leaves inside a book until they are flat and dry (2-3 days). Then place them between a sheet of folded wax paper and iron. Create a leaf guide specific to your geographic area by compiling the pressed leaves and written descriptions into a book.

DESIGN A PET

Taxonomy is the area of science that deals with classifying living things. Display pictures of animals with unique features such as a platypus, an octopus, or a bat. Ask students to name animals they resemble (e.g., a platypus has a bill like a duck but fur like a beaver, while a bat has wings like a bird and fur like a mouse). Then have them clip pictures of animals from magazines. On chart paper, list the different physical features of the animals, such as tentacles, shells, gills, fur, antennae, wings, feathers, and scales. Encourage kids to select and arrange the features to create an outrageous pet. Have them draw a sketch and write about the accommodations they would need to make in their homes to care for these pets.

CURRICULUM CONNECTIONS

MATH: Guess the Rule

YOU'LL NEED: attribute blocks, 3 Hula Hoops, index cards

Use Venn diagrams to help students classify the attributes of geometric shapes and figures. Arrange two different-colored Hula Hoops so they are overlapping. Use blocks with at least four attributes (such as color, size, shape, and material) to play a game called "Guess the Rule." First, demonstrate the game by sorting a few blocks within the Venn diagram. Using index cards label one hoop "Blue Blocks" and the other "Small Blocks." Ask kids to place the remaining blocks into the hoops using the criteria on the cards. Then move all small blue blocks to the center of the overlapping hoops (to show that they meet both criteria). Next, ask them to guess the rule for sorting a set such as "circles" in one hoop and "yellow blocks" in another. This time, place a few shapes inside the hoops without using index cards. Ask kids to notice the attributes. Then challenge them to correctly place a block within the hoops and tell them whether it meets the rule or not. Work with smaller groups to sort the blocks according to more complicated relationships, such as yellow or red in one hoop, wooden in the second, and squares in a third. Vary the activity by adding pattern blocks or other figures.

RESOURCES

WEB SITE

www.treeguide.com Log on for a complete guide to the world's trees, by list or dichotomous key.

BOOKS

National Geographic Animal Encyclopedia (National Geographic Society, 2000).

Trees: Trees Identified by Leaf, Bark, & Seed by Steven M. L. Aronson (Fandex Family Field Guides, 1998).

SOFTWARE

Logical Journey of the Zoombinis (Broderbund) A math program which focuses on attributes, patterns, sorting, and grouping.

BACK TO "BASE"-ICS

A+ Activities

WHY WE LIKE THIS ACTIVITY

*T*his science activity is a low-cost, visual way to introduce acids and bases. It uses materials with which students are already familiar to acquaint them with a difficult concept.

*M*y students enjoy using supplies that they find in their kitchens to do science experiments. One of their favorite projects is using cabbage and coffee filters to make litmus paper for testing acids and bases (also called alkalis). To prepare for this activity, I make cabbage water ahead of time (see right). Students then dip coffee filters (one at a time) into the juice, which turns them light blue. After the filters have dried on a cookie sheet or newspaper, students cut the dried filters into wide strips. I fill small jars with familiar liquids, such as lemon juice, pickle juice, vinegar, and milk. Then students dip the testing strips into the liquids. If a light blue strip turns greenish, the liquid is a base, and if it turns pinkish-red, the liquid is an acid. Students write the name of the liquid at the top of each test strip and tape it to a bulletin board to make a "rainbow" from the most acidic to the most basic (alkaline) liquids.

—*Joann Jacobs*
Nashville, TN

ADAPTING UP OR DOWN

FOR YOUNGER GRADES

*W*hen students test various liquids, ask them to place the test strips in two categories: acids or bases. They can then place them in Venn diagrams to show their similarities and differences, such as "acids and foods" or "bases and cleaning supplies."

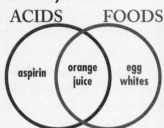

ACIDS   FOODS

aspirin | orange juice | egg whites

RESOURCES

WEB SITES

www.coaleducation.org/lessons/primary/properties/ph.htm This lesson plan for grades 3-8 is about acids, bases, and pH.

www.delta-ed.com Purchase a pH meter, acid rain study kits, and other supplies at Delta Education. For more information, call (800) 442-5444.

www.miamisci.org/ph/ Students and teachers can log on for easy-to-follow experiments about pH.

BOOKS

Chemistry for Every Kid by Janice VanCleave (John Wiley & Sons, 1989).

Kitchen Science Experiments by Barbara Saffer (Lowell House, 2000).

The Science Factory by Jon Richards (Copper Beech, 2000).

What Can I Do? The Science Spiders Learn Acid-Base Chemistry by Kathleen E. Kain (Ranch Works, 1999).

TAKING IT FURTHER

INDICATE THE BEST INDICATOR

*I*n addition to cabbage, many other fruits and vegetables (such as blackberries, blueberries, cherries, onions, and beets) can be used to make acid/base indicators. (Due to a chemical reaction, their dyes turn a distinctive color when combined with acids or bases.) Have students make testing strips from these fruits and vegetables. They can then test liquids using various types of testing strips to see which indicator is the clearest to read. Also provide students with manufactured litmus paper (check pet or pool-supply stores) or a pH meter (see Resources, left). Students can then compare the readings of the manufactured litmus papers with their homemade indicators. Ask students: *When would you use pH tests?* (to test fish tank water, swimming pools, rain water, soil, etc.) *Which type of indicator do you think is the most accurate? Ones made from fruits and vegetables or manufactured readers? Why?*

creative classroom

How to Make CABBAGE WATER

YOU'LL NEED: one red cabbage, water, cooking pot, stove, bowl

★ Cut the cabbage into small pieces and place them in a pot of water.
★ Bring to a boil, then let simmer for about 10 minutes.
★ Remove the mixture from the heat and let stand for about one hour.
★ Pour off the liquid into a separate bowl and discard the cabbage.

Cabbage water may be stored in a closed jar in the refrigerator.

CURRICULUM CONNECTIONS

ART: Coloring with Cabbage

YOU'LL NEED: Cabbage water (see below), blotting paper, paintbrushes, small jars of various liquids representing acids and bases (vinegar, coffee, milk, dishwashing liquid, soda, lemon juice, pickle juice, tomato juice, etc.)

Have students dip the blotting paper into the cabbage water and place the sheets on newspapers or hang to dry. Students can then experiment with color by using various acids and bases to "paint" pictures on the cabbage-stained blotting paper. If a student paints with a base, the paper will turn blue or green. If a student paints with an acid, the paper will turn red or pink.

MATH: Make a Bar Graph

YOU'LL NEED: Litmus paper, baby food jars with lids, various acids and bases, index cards, markers

Provide each child with one baby food jar or other small jar with a lid and a Zip-Loc plastic bag. As a homework assignment, ask students to work with their parents to fill the jar with a liquid found around their home, such as dishwashing liquid, coffee, orange juice, or a kid-safe household detergent. Then ask them to label the jar, place it in the plastic bag, seal it, and bring it to school. Each student can use litmus paper or a pH meter to test the liquid, then label the strip with its pH value (number). Have each student tape the litmus paper to an index card and write the name of the substance. Have students work together to make a bar graph of the values of the substances from most acidic to most basic. Extend this activity by bringing in some additional liquids that you have identified with labels. Before testing these new liquids, ask students to predict their pH value. Then have students test each substance to see if their predictions were accurate.

MEETING THE STANDARDS

NATIONAL SCIENCE EDUCATION STANDARDS
Physical Science—Properties and Changes of Properties in Matter

A substance has characteristic properties, all of which are independent of the amount of the sample. Substances are often placed in categories or groups if they react in similar ways.

SPARK CREATIVITY

OUR OWN CALENDAR

At the end of each month, I ask my students to help me create next month's calendar. I give each student a square piece of card stock to create his or her own seasonal picture (e.g., a snow scene for January or a heart for February). I introduce students to a different art technique each month, such as "tear art," oil pastels, water-colors, and so on. When the cards are done, I write students' names along the bottoms and a date of the month in the top corner. Then I clip them to our large calendar board. During our daily morning meetings, the student who created that day's card gets to lead the class in saying the date.

—Carrie-Anne Gray
Danville, CA

SPIFF UP YOUR SCHOOL

As the school year drew to a close last June, my fourth-graders decided to leave a last-ing impression. With the help of a local artist, kids designed and painted murals on the dreary cement planters in our courtyard. They signed and dated each planter. Because the students' artwork will brighten up our school and be admired for years to come, I plan to ask future classes to come up with similar year-end beauti-fication projects.

—Susanna Stratford
South San Francisco, CA

FEELING THE SEASON

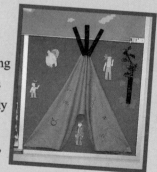

My multiply impaired students especially enjoy the three-dimensional Thanksgiving bulletin board we create together. The textures and movement of the pieces on the board really help them "feel" the season. We paint paper-towel tubes to construct log cabins and tepees, use sticks and silk leaves to make trees, fill a garbage bag with shredded paper to represent Plymouth Rock, and finger paint ocean waves. I then attach the items to the board with Velcro so that kids can remove the pieces and touch them for tactile stimulation. Though they may not fully understand the concept of Thanksgiving, my students "feel" that they are part of the holiday.

—Donna McGovern
Palos Hills, IL

Coloring for a Cause

My students learn about giving by creating a "money-raising" color-ing book. As a class, we write a story and each student illustrates a page in "coloring book" style (i.e., drawing only the outlines of the pictures). We then put the pages in order and copy them to create color-ing books. At the school's annual holiday bazaar, we sell them for one dollar each and donate the proceeds to the school for literacy projects.

—Mary Bolte
Mansfield, OH

She dropped them off at their hollow bamboo tree on the forest floor.

"Mom's" the Word

My students (and their mothers) love this new twist on the traditional Mother's Day card. A week before the holiday, kids draw portraits of their moms and also make medieval-looking scrolls from butcher paper. Both portraits and scrolls are hung on a bulletin board. Then each day that week, students write thoughtful sentences about their mothers on their scrolls (e.g., "I love when my mom sings to me"). We invite mothers to visit our classroom to enjoy the work in progress. On Friday, children roll up their scrolls, tie them up with a ribbon, and take them home with the portraits. Moms appreciate the meaningful Mother's Day gifts.

—*Judy Meagher*
Bozeman, MT

Creative Costume Corner

When my students arrive at school each morning, they look forward to using our dramatic-play station. In our Costume Corner, I have suitcases packed with assorted clothes, hats, and shoes—everything kids need to dress up as chefs, fairy princesses, cowboys, and more. To compile such an assortment of costumes, I purchase inexpensive clothing at thrift shops. I also send letters home in mid-October asking parents and students to donate their costumes after Halloween. It's amazing how a few costumes and props can help broaden kids' imaginations.

—*Linda DiPasquale-Morello*
Buena, NJ

Without a Shadow of a Doubt

My students enjoy predicting if the groundhog will see its shadow on Groundhog Day (February 2). They begin by writing a prediction on a slip of paper and pasting it on half of a white paper plate. Next, they create a sun by cutting out triangles along the edge of a yellow paper plate. They staple the half plate (with the prediction) to the yellow sun plate to make a pocket. Then they make groundhogs from toilet paper tubes, brown paper, and felt, and fit them in the paper plate pockets. To complete the project, children who predict that spring is just around the corner glue white cloud shapes on their yellow "sun" plates to indicate that the groundhog will *not* see his shadow. Without a shadow of a doubt, this is one of my students' favorite projects.

—*Gail E. Sherwood*
Chicago, IL

ADD COLOR

Create a space where kids can express themselves. Cover a wall in your classroom with brown paper and leave a supply of colorful markers and crayons nearby. Encourage students to draw, write favorite sayings, and leave messages for one another. For an added burst of color, have students paint the garbage pails in your classroom and around the school.

—*Amy Rubin*
Los Angeles, CA

Mirror, Mirror, on the Wall

I found an enchanting way to help students memorize poems. I created a "stage-door" mirror by fastening three floor-length mirrors into a triangular shape. I then decorated the frames with stickers, buttons, shimmering paper, beads, and colorful tape. I have students stand in front of the magical mirror as they recite poems. It's really helped turn my students onto poetry.

—*Bill Walker*
Jackson, TN

ILLUSTRATION: ANDY LEVINE

A+ activities

ON THEIR BEST

Toeing the Line

I added a twist to the same old routine of lining up. To encourage students to line up in an organized manner, we play a guessing game. I give them clues to help them guess the identity of a mystery student. I start with a big category, such as, "I'm thinking of a girl." Any student who *doesn't* fit the category (in this case, every boy) joins the line. Gradually, I narrow down the clues so that the description only fits two or three kids and then, finally, just one! This game encourages my first-graders to pay attention to details and to join the line at the appropriate time.

— Jon Harper
Secretary, MD

Having kids line up in an orderly fashion was always a problem until I tried this new trick! I cut "footprints" from colored construction paper (a pair for each student), and numbered them. I fastened the footprints to the floor by covering them with wide transparent tape, each pair a few steps apart from the next. When it is time to line up, I call each student's name and ask him or her to stand on a certain footprint. This not only helps things run smoothly at line-up time, it reinforces color and number recognition.

—Sondra Lougee
Port Monmouth, NJ

ENCORE!

While waiting to be dismissed for lunch or home, my students take "curtain calls." I made a curtain by stapling a piece of fabric to a yardstick and added tassels to make it look theatrical. As kids line up, I pick a name out of a hat to determine who will perform for the class. I then hold the curtain in front of the chosen student and announce what he or she has decided to do (e.g., recite a rhyme, tell a joke, do a dance, etc.). Next I lift up the curtain and rest it behind the student as a backdrop while he or she performs. This activity transforms time that was once wasted into an opportunity for each student to be a star.

—Judy Meagher
Bozeman, MT

Accentuate the Positive

We turn discipline into a positive learning experience. If a student breaks a rule, he or she fills out a Behavior Card. The card includes the student's name, the date, "What I was doing wrong," "Why this was wrong," and "What I should have been doing." This action not only encourages students to consider what the positive behavior should have been, but the cards give us documentation in the student's handwriting for parent/teacher conferences.

—Ellen Auten
Indianapolis, IN

Huh?

Have you ever had five children approach you with *the exact same question?* To help students find out answers on their own, I've developed the rule "see three before me." Before asking me a question, a child must ask three classmates for help and get their signatures on a slip of paper. Not only has this system taught kids to solve problems without my help, it also provides a great way for them to learn from one another.

—Catherine Charles
Los Angeles, CA

BEHAVIOR

See You Tomorrow!

I keep my students on their toes and my classroom neat with this simple dismissal tip. As students line up to leave, they must tell me something they learned in class that day and show me a piece of trash they picked up from the floor or are throwing out to tidy their desks. My floors are spotless and my students are ready to respond to their parents' inevitable question: "What did you learn in school today?"

—Elsa Noble
West Palm Beach, FL

Here's a tip that works wonders for dismissal. Each morning I write a "Joke of the Day" on the chalkboard. Students read it and try to think of possible punch lines. Just before the bell rings at the end of the day, kids share punch lines they came up with, and then I reveal the answer. It's a fun way to end the day on a positive note.

—Kathy Clarke
San Antonio, TX

TATTLE NO MORE!

To curb tattling—which took away from precious teaching time—I labeled a plain cardboard box "complaints." Now, instead of approaching me to tell me about problems with classmates, students write what happened on a slip of paper and place the slip in the complaint box. Several times a day I empty the box and confer with students. I also have kids write down good deeds they see in the classroom and place their praise in a nicely decorated box labeled "compliments." At the end of the week, I deliver the complimentary messages to students. There usually are several messages in the box for me, too!

—Heather Mitchell
Hallandale, FL

To curb tattling, I devised this simple phrase: "IN OR OUT?" I ask the child, "Are you telling me this to get your classmate IN trouble or OUT of danger?" I listen to students only if the answer is "OUT" of danger. Now kids think twice before they tattle.

—Peggy Campbell-Rush
Hampton, NJ

WATCH THE LIGHT

To decrease discipline problems I made a poster of a traffic light and wrote each student's name on a clothespin. At the beginning of the day, I clip all the clothespins around the edge of the green light. If a student acts up during the day, I move his or her clip to the yellow light, and, if the behavior continues, I move it to the red light and take appropriate disciplinary action. To reward students who have stayed on the green light all week, I pass out "green people treats," such as bookmarks and pencils.

—Skila Brown
Durham, NC

KEEPING SPIRITS

ON TARGET

I've found a great way to motivate my students to improve their grades. After each report card, I explain to students and parents that the child's average for each subject is a new target for improvement. On each assignment and test where the child earns a grade higher than that subject's target number, I stamp a star. For example, a student who earned a 72 percent on the previous report card will receive a star for a 73 percent or higher. Target numbers are individualized and allow all students to feel successful.

—*Jan Shaffer*
Plainfield, IN

Phone Home

I've found that positive phone calls can motivate my students. Every Tuesday, I choose a student in my class who has shown leadership, initiative, or responsibility, and I write a brief description of what the child did and what qualities the action exhibited. I then give the description to the principal who awards the student with a blue ribbon and calls the child's family to relay the good news.

—*Linda Barrett*
Spencer, IN

I SECOND THAT EMOTION

Many of my kindergartners have difficulty verbalizing their emotions. To help them explain their feelings, I made a poster with faces (cut from magazines) that have different expressions (happy, sad, tired, mad, excited, etc.). I hung the poster at the entrance to my classroom. Now, as I greet students in the morning, each one points to the face that best describes his or her mood. This lets me know how kids are feeling each morning.

—*Mitchell Rigby*
Newark, NJ

Eliminate the Negative

Every Monday, to set the tone for the week, I hang a positive quote on my bulletin board. I post such gems as, "The only place where success comes before work is in the dictionary," "Don't wait for your ship to come in—swim out to it," and "Don't be afraid to climb out on a limb—that's where the fruit is." We then take a few minutes to reflect on how the quote can motivate us to strive for specific goals that we've set as a class. At the end of the week, I put the words of wisdom into a class book which I'll photocopy and give to each student at the end of the year. I never run out of great quotes because my students often bring in ones they've heard or read.

—*Craig Lubich*
Prescott, WI

Oops!

We all makes mistakes! To prove this point to kids and to encourage them to reread their work, I make up special handouts called Oops Pages! They contain errors in spelling, punctuation, grammar, history facts, or math problems. I tell kids that I forgot to use my "spell check," mixed up historical dates, or forgot to add the decimal point when multiplying. Kids look forward to locating and correcting all of my errors. And they learn that the only error in making a mistake is leaving it uncorrected!

—*Stephanie Sabatino*
Philadelphia, PA

HIGH

A MAGIC SEND-OFF

As students file out of my classroom at the end of the day, I like to give them a little love to send them on their way. So I've created a "magic carpet" featuring four color squares: a heart, which represents a hug; a hand, which means a handshake; a smiley face, which stands for a big smile; and the number five, which means a high five. As each student leaves, he or she steps on one of the squares, and I give him or her the chosen send-off. It's a positive way to cap off the day!

—*Dawn Ingram*
Cottonwood, AL

CANDID CAMERA

I get my students to follow classroom rules by capturing them in the act! Whenever I see a student modeling good behavior—helping others, cleaning an area, or reading a book quietly—I snap an instant photo! I then tack the photo (along with the student's name, the date, and a description of the behavior) to a bulletin board. This "quick click" acknowledges well-behaved students and encourages others to follow classroom procedures.

—*Janis Ramson*
Wheeling, WV

The Lunch Bunch

Each Tuesday, I invite one student to join me for lunch in our classroom. I write each child's name on a sheet of paper that I designed to look like a lunch tray. I keep the sheets in a brown-paper lunch bag and randomly choose one each week. I keep the sheets of the students I've already lunched with in a folder. Once each child has had a turn, I start over. We've all enjoyed having this special time to get to know one another.

—*Lauren Treinish*
Philadelphia, PA

COMING SOON...

When completing a unit in any given curriculum area, I like to get my students guessing about what will come next. I start by giving a few clues. For instance, I might play "The Battle Hymn of the Republic" prior to a lesson on the American Civil War. I share such clues with the class each day during the morning meeting and then give kids an opportunity to talk among themselves and speculate about what they will be studying next. Kids share their ideas by writing them on chart paper. Having gained important background knowledge, my students are already anticipating the next unit.

—*Tami Frediani*
Fresno, CA

Get-well Wishes

When one of my students misses school because of a long-term illness, an injury, or surgery, I have my class use fabric markers to decorate a plain pillowcase with drawings, greetings, and signatures. We then send the get-well pillowcase to the absent student. Every moment the ill child spends in bed is made a little easier with these warm wishes from classmates.

—*Julia Alarie*
Essex, VT

creative classroom

59

A+ activities

MAKE THE SCHOOL/

INVITE PARENTS TO LUNCH

My fourth-graders designed an Author's Get-Away Café where, during my planning period from 12 to 1 p.m., they make reservations to eat lunch with their parents. The "café" looks like a charming patio overlooking the ocean. While classical music plays softly, students and their guests enjoy a quiet lunch that they bring from the cafeteria. Afterward, students share their writing portfolios with parents, and I talk about my writing program. The café is booked solid every week and gets rave reviews from its "customers."

—*Barbara Glinski*
Titusville, FL

Don't Forget the Good News!

When I noticed that most of my notes home to parents were about problems—and that students' report cards didn't paint the whole picture—I decided to get out the good news. Every other month I send each parent a positive postcard. In just a few lines, I highlight positive behavior, marked improvement, and other actions that shouldn't go unnoticed. On alternate months, I give parents a positive phone call. Moms and dads always thank me for sharing the good news.

—*Pam Tabor*
Miami, FL

SELF-PORTRAIT STATIONERY

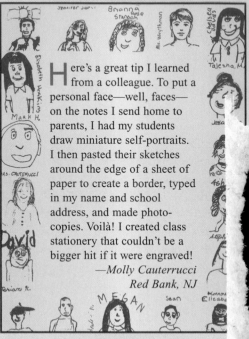

Here's a great tip I learned from a colleague. To put a personal face—well, faces—on the notes I send home to parents, I had my students draw miniature self-portraits. I then pasted their sketches around the edge of a sheet of paper to create a border, typed in my name and school address, and made photocopies. Voilà! I created class stationery that couldn't be a bigger hit if it were engraved!

—*Molly Cauterrucci*
Red Bank, NJ

Class Web Site

I've created a Web site to keep parents informed about what's going on in our classroom. (To learn how to create a class Web site, visit **www.teachervision.com** and click on "Class Webcreate.") I keep it simple—it's only one page long—but I update the information on the first day of every month and include upcoming classroom events, themes we are studying, details about long-term assignments, and some safe links to Web sites related to topics in my curriculum. Our Web site also has a link to my e-mail so that parents can contact me. The site has really helped open up the lines of communication between parents and me.

—*Genevieve Petrillo*
Belleville, NJ
http://members.aol.com/Smoki2/page1.html

Good News Travels Fast

There's nothing like a public library filled with diligent students to help get the good news out to the community about our classroom activities. When my students begin their research for class projects, I plan a voluntary Saturday afternoon or after-school research day at our public library. (Parent volunteers help me arrange a car pool so that all students who wish to attend can be there.) While I point my students in the direction of great research material and answer questions, I also get the chance to chat with parents and community members about everything that's going on at school. This provides a great forum for talking about what's *right* with our school.

—*Steven Vetter*
Brooksville, FL

HOME CONNECTION

PARENT PAGES

To help children learn to communicate with their families about school, I create inter- active home-

work assignments. These assignments have questions that parents ask their children about what's going on at school. One assign- ment might read, "Today we learned about measurement. Ask your child: What things did you measure at school? How did you measure them?" Interactive homework also includes activities parents and kids can do together (e.g., "Measure the smallest person in your family.") Kids and parents both seem to enjoy working and learning together.

—Judy Meagher
Bozeman, MT

WANTED: PARENTS AT SCHOOL

Our eye-catching back-to-school-night bul- letin board, "Wanted: You At School," really encouraged parents to get involved. On the board, we highlighted things parents can

do to be part of their child's education, such as attending school events, supporting school rules, reading with their child, volun- teering, and keeping in touch with teachers. We then stapled a shiny party tray in the center of the board to act as a mirror so that parents could see themselves getting involved—and it worked!

—Nancy Dentler
Mobile, AL

Neighborhood of Names

To help visiting parents recognize and find teachers when they visit our school, we created a welcoming bulletin board in our lobby. The board, titled "Mr. Archer's Neighborhood" (Mr. Archer is our principal), fea- tures a friendly car-filled street lined with houses. On the cars and houses, we glued pictures of the teachers and wrote their names and room numbers. It's a

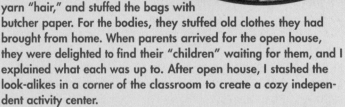

great "neighborly" way to help parents find the right rooms when they visit our school!

—Lori Christopoulos & Angie Castleberry
Tulsa, OK

Stuffed Shirts

For our spring open house, my third- and fourth-graders created life-size replicas of themselves to place in our room "doing" their favorite activities— working on the computer, reading, and drawing pictures. To make the look- alikes, kids drew self-por- traits on paper bags, added yarn "hair," and stuffed the bags with

butcher paper. For the bodies, they stuffed old clothes they had brought from home. When parents arrived for the open house, they were delighted to find their "children" waiting for them, and I explained what each was up to. After open house, I stashed the look-alikes in a corner of the classroom to create a cozy indepen- dent activity center.

—Cynthia Shubert
Lompoc, CA

Connect with Parents

I like to keep in touch with parents every week—not just at par- ent-teacher conferences—so I created a "Friday Folder." Every Friday, I send home a folder with students' work from the week and a brief note about what we did. Most importantly, perhaps, is the response card that parents can complete and send back to me with their comments and questions. On special holidays, students like to surprise parents by including a handmade card in the folder.

—Jennifer Smith
Columbus, OH

SEASONAL ★ KIDS' PAGES

*D*o you have trouble finding new and innovative ways to teach about seasonal themes and special events? Your troubles are over! These special Kids' Pages offer fresh and timely ways to spiff up your lessons throughout the year. They begin with back-to-school topics such as friendship and continue with holidays and events, including Halloween, Hispanic Heritage Month, Black History Month, Chinese New Year, Presidents' Day, Women's History Month, and Earth Day.

These quick and easy reproducibles will help students acquire and reinforce important basic concepts and skills including problem solving, reading comprehension, cultural connections, mapping, symmetry, graphing, and using graphic organizers. They even include recipes and a play!

Far from drill-and-practice busywork, these Kids' Pages engage students in activities, projects, and higher-order thinking. Some will spark great discussions and others will inspire students to learn more on their own. And they will all be a welcome addition to your class's understanding of seasonal themes and events.

Passport to Friendship

Cut out the pages on the dotted lines and put them in order.
Staple the pages together, and then fill in the blanks.

My
PASSPORT

to
Friendship

My name is _____. ❶

I am _____ years old.

I live in _____.

I like to _____

_____

_____.

Here is a picture of me:

❷

I am a good friend when I _____

_____

and when I _____

_____.

Here is a picture of me being a good friend:

❸

Here are my friends' names!

❹

ILLUSTRATION: BRUCE VAN PATTER

Find a Friendly Ending

Read the comic strip and then answer the following questions. (You can write your answers on the back of this paper.)

1. What is the problem in the comic strip?

2. How do you think each kid feels?

3. What might happen if the kids don't work out the problem?

4. What are at least two ways the kids can solve the problem?

Now draw your own ending to the story in the last box.

How can Sarah and Jake solve the problem? Draw and write about what you think should happen next.

Name _____

ILLUSTRATIONS: BRUCE VAN PATTER

What Kind of Friend Are You?

Do you have what it takes to be a perfect pal? Find out by taking this friendship quiz. Circle the letter that best describes what you would do in each situation.

1. **While visiting your friend's house, you spot her diary sitting out on her desk. Your friend is out of the room. You:**

   A. read as much as you can before she comes back.

   B. ignore it, except for a brief glance down to make sure your name is not there.

   C. ignore it, and point it out to your friend when she returns (since you know she has nosy brothers and sisters).

2. **You catch your friend smoking in the bathroom—for the second time. You:**

   A. stick around and try the cigarette your friend offers you.

   B. talk to an adult you trust about your concerns.

   C. pretend you didn't see anything.

3. **You did not do your math homework last night, but you know your buddy is a whiz at fractions. You:**

   A. copy your friend's answers while he is not paying attention.

   B. ask your buddy if you can borrow his answers and promise a favor in return.

   C. face the consequences for not doing your homework, but ask your friend to give you a math lesson later.

4. **You are invited to play basketball with the most popular kids at school—but your best pal is not. You:**

   A. jump at the chance to go, and ignore the hurt look on your friend's face. (After all, you are not the one making the plans.)

   B. tell the kids who invited you how much fun your pal is, and ask if she can come along.

   C. go for a while, then leave to spend some time with your pal.

5. **Your pal's parents recently announced they are getting a divorce. Now it is all your friend can talk about. You:**

   A. start making excuses for why you can't hang out with your friend as much as you used to.

   B. gently tell your friend that you would like to talk about other, more interesting topics.

   C. listen when your friend needs to talk, and suggest that he see the school guidance counselor.

6. **There's a new girl in your class who just moved to the U.S. from a different country. You:**

   A. giggle when other kids make fun of the girl's accent.

   B. smile at the new girl and invite her to join you at lunch.

   C. ignore the new girl AND the kids who are making fun of her.

7. **You and your friend get into an argument over the rules of a board game. You:**

   A. tell your friend to get lost if he can't play by your rules.

   B. wait until your friend says he is sorry, then admit you were being unreasonable, too.

   C. apologize for your part in the disagreement and suggest another game.

SCORE YOURSELF!

Follow your teacher's directions to score your quiz. My score is _____.

How did you rate?

✖ If you scored **0 to 4 points**, you have some work to do. Stop thinking about yourself and try putting yourself in your pal's place.

✖ If you scored **5 to 9 points**, you're on the right track. You are usually a caring friend, but you may need to work on being more loyal.

✖ If you scored **10 to 14 points**, congratulations! You know how to treat a friend and are a good role model for others to follow.

Name _____

ILLUSTRATION: BRUCE VAN PATTER

Marvin's Misery

The beginning of the school year is a time to put your best foot forward. For most of us, it's a time to wear our favorite clothes, carry new school supplies, and get set to learn. Read this story about Marvin, a boy who didn't exactly start off on the right foot. Then answer the questions below. If you need more room, use the back of this page.

It all started when Marvin stayed up late on a school night to finish a juicy mystery called *Blue Slime in the Attic*. But poor Marvin! Just as he got to the end of the book, he realized that the last page was missing. That made Marvin's mind race all night.

When his alarm clock rang in the morning, Marvin accidentally flung it across the room. It went through the open window and hit Marvin's father on the head as he was going out the back door. Marvin had to spend ten minutes apologizing to his father.

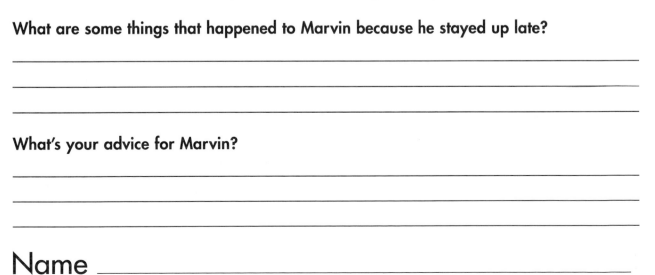

Since Marvin was running so late, he decided he didn't really need to wash, brush his teeth, or comb his hair. In fact, Marvin just slipped on the clothes he had worn the day before. When Marvin's mother told him that he needed to eat a healthy breakfast before school, Marvin said he had no time.

When Marvin got to school, he felt weird, as if his body was made of marshmallow and his brain had been baked in an oven. He had no energy, and his friends kept asking him if he was all right.

Marvin's friend, Lucinda, took one look at him and said, "What happened to you? You look like you spent the night in a closet!" And Leo, Marvin's pal from the first grade, whispered, "Marv, buddy, you've got stinky breath!"

By 11 o'clock, Marvin couldn't keep his eyes open or his head up anymore. His head, covered with a mass of greasy curls, actually fell onto the desk in the middle of math class. As the other students learned long division, Marvin slept soundly. Poor Marvin.

What are some things that happened to Marvin because he stayed up late?

_____

_____

_____

What's your advice for Marvin?

_____

_____

_____

Name _____

A Spooky Crossword

Read the clues carefully, and then fill in the crossword.

Down

1. A warlock casts a magic _____.

2. One who has magic powers.

4. It can be scary, sad, or happy, and it is worn over your face.

6. The type of feline that is most often connected with this day.

8. An invisible spirit.

9. It lives in caves, hangs upside down, and can fly.

Across

3. It is needed if you're going to make a jack-o'-lantern.

5. It's not very pretty, it's thought to be evil, and it pals around with ghosts.

7. Wolves sometimes do this at a full moon.

9. What a ghost says to scare you.

10. It can be held to sweep or used to fly.

11. Trick or _____.

12. On this night, people sometimes visit _____ houses.

Now write a story incorporating all 13 words. Begin the story with, "Mystic, my black cat, purred at my window pane on Halloween night. As the wind howled, I hurried to take off my skeleton costume. But the problem was, the costume would not come off. It was as if it was glued to my body. I didn't know what to do, so I . . ."

Name _____

ILLUSTRATIONS: BRUCE VAN PATTER

68

Details, Details

This year, Kyle Thomas wants to host a Halloween party, but he needs some help with the details. Help him decide in what order he should do things. First, read all of the items on the things-to-do list. Then number them in the order you think they should get done. (There isn't one "right" way of planning the party—just try to be logical and efficient.)

Things to do

☐ Thank family for their help in making the party a scary success.

☐ Fill trick-or-treat bags to give guests as they leave.

☐ Go to grocery store to buy refreshments.

☐ Go to bank to get money to pay for the party.

☐ Greet guests.

☐ Give out trick-or-treat bags.

☐ Put on costume.

☐ Ask a friend to help host the party.

☐ Write a guest list.

☐ Bake skeleton cookies for the party.

☐ Think of a costume.

☐ Make a fruity punch.

☐ Make spooky decorations.

☐ Send out invitations.

☐ Make invitations.

☐ Clean the house from top to bottom.

☐ Ask parents permission to have the party.

☐ Hang bats, skeletons, and other decorations.

☐ Cover the table with an orange-and-black table cloth.

☐ Pour the punch into the punch bowl and don't forget the ice.

Yum, Yum

Invent a **Halloween Punch** recipe for the party. Write the ingredients on the back of this page. Share your recipe with the rest of the class. Which of your classmates' recipes would you like to try?

ILLUSTRATIONS: BRUCE VAN PATTER

Name _____

Language Look-alikes

Some English and Spanish words look alike. Read each Spanish word below. Find the English word from the box that looks the same or almost the same and write it on the line. Then write the English words in the crossword puzzle.

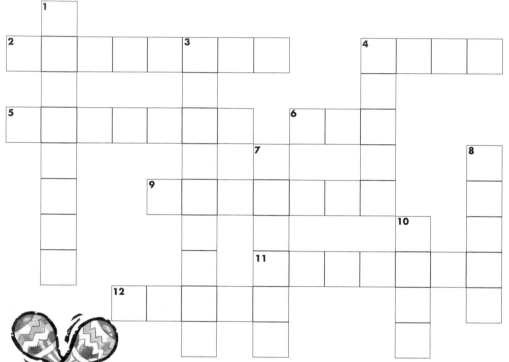

ENGLISH WORD BOX

park
soup
map
airport
October
paper
tomato
bicycle
plate
fruit
calendar
families
delicious

DOWN

1. Las familias (lahs fah-MEE-lee-ahs)
_____

3. Delicioso (deh-lee-si-OH-soh)
_____

4. El papel (ell pah-PEL)
_____

7. El tomate (ell toh-MAH-teh)
_____

8. El plato (ell PLAH-toh)
_____

10. La sopa (lah SOH-pah)
_____

ACROSS

2. El calendario (ell kah-lehn-DAH-re-yoh)
_____

4. El parque (ell PAHR-keh)
_____

5. La bicicleta (lah bee-see-KLEH-tah)
_____

6. El mapa (ell MAH-pah)
_____

9. Octubre (ok-TOO-breh)
_____

11. El aeropuerto (ell ah-eh-roh-PWEHR-toh)
_____

12. La fruta (lah FROO-tah)
_____

Name _____

Make a Folktale Mini-Book!

1. Color the pictures.
2. Cut out the pages.

3. Put them in order.
4. Staple them together.

Rabbit's Race
A Mexican Folktale

Rabbit and Frog lived long
ago in Mexico.

One day, Rabbit bragged that he was
the fastest one in the land.
Frog said, "Let's have a race!"

The two animals raced to the river.
Rabbit ran fast. Frog hopped slowly.

But Frog had help. Frog's friends
were hiding in the grass. One by one, they
leaped out in front of Rabbit.
They looked just like Frog.

Rabbit was confused. No matter how
fast Rabbit ran, Frog always seemed
to be one leap ahead of him!

Finally, the animals reached the river.
With the help of his friends, Frog won the
race. And Rabbit never bragged again.
THE END

ILLUSTRATIONS: BRUCE VAN PATTER

71

Traveling the Americas

Latin Americans come to the United States from many places. Many Hispanics come from Mexico, Puerto Rico, Cuba, El Salvador, and the Dominican Republic. These places are highlighted on the map below. Study the map, and then answer the questions.

1. What body of water forms a natural boundary between the United States and Mexico?

   ❑ a. The Pacific Ocean
   ❑ b. The Caribbean Sea
   ❑ c. The Rio Grande
   ❑ d. The Atlantic Ocean

2. Which of these places is farthest east?

   ❑ a. Cuba
   ❑ b. Puerto Rico
   ❑ c. The Dominican Republic
   ❑ d. Mexico

3. Which of these places are islands?

   ❑ a. Cuba
   ❑ b. Puerto Rico
   ❑ c. The Dominican Republic
   ❑ d. All of the above

4. If a person were traveling from the Dominican Republic to the southeastern tip of the United States, in which direction would the person go?

   ❑ a. Northeast   ❑ b. Southeast
   ❑ c. Northwest   ❑ d. Southwest

ILLUSTRATION: BRUCE VAN PATTER

Name _____

Is That a Fact?

A **FACT** is a statement that can be proved true. An **OPINION** is a statement that tells how a person thinks or feels about something. It cannot be proved true. Read each sentence about Christopher Columbus. Then circle **F** for fact or **O** for opinion.

Example:

FACT: Columbus was born in Italy.

OPINION: Columbus was the smartest man who ever lived.

F O 1. Christopher Columbus was braver than most other explorers.

F O 2. The United States of America should be named after Christopher Columbus.

F O 3. Columbus set sail in 1492.

F O 4. Columbus was greedier than most explorers.

F O 5. Columbus's three ships were the *Nina*, the *Pinta*, and the *Santa Maria*.

F O 6. Columbus and his crew sailed west across the Atlantic Ocean.

F O 7. Columbus's voyage across the Atlantic took more than a month.

F O 8. Columbus is a hero.

F O 9. Columbus is a villain.

F O 10. According to his logs, Columbus believed he had reached the Indies.

F O 11. Columbus must not have been very intelligent, since he did not realize he had landed in North America.

F O 12. Spain's Queen Isabella and King Ferdinand paid for Columbus's voyage.

F O 13. The second Monday in October is Columbus Day, a national holiday.

F O 14. Americans should stop celebrating Columbus Day, since Columbus did not really discover America.

ILLUSTRATIONS: BRUCE VAN PATTER

Name _____

Mmm, Math!

The Pilgrims made golden corn bread to eat. You can, too!
Look at this recipe; then answer the questions.

CORN BREAD

This recipe makes 30 miniature corn bread muffins.

You will need:
- ✔ 1 cup cornmeal
- ✔ 1 1/2 cups whole wheat flour
- ✔ 4 cups water
- ✔ 1 teaspoon salt

What to do:
1. Put the cornmeal and water in a large pot.
2. Bring the pot to a boil. Lower the heat and cook for half an hour. Stir every few minutes.
3. Mix the flour and salt with the hot cornmeal.
4. Using an ice cream scoop, put mounds of the mixture on a cookie sheet.
5. Put the cookie sheet in an oven heated to 375 degrees. Bake for 15 minutes. Turn corn breads over and bake for another 10 minutes.

1. How much salt do you need to make this recipe?

_____

2. Which do you need more of: cornmeal or water?

_____

3. What is the first step you follow to make corn bread?

_____
_____
_____
_____
_____

4. The corn bread muffins bake for 15 minutes on one side and 10 minutes on the other side. How long do they bake altogether?

_____

BONUS: How many children are in your class? _____ If you followed this recipe, would you have enough corn bread muffins for everyone? _____

Name _____

CELEBRATE THE SANDWICH!

In honor of the Earl of Sandwich, make a sandwich flip book. Cut out the rectangles below. Stack the pictures in order with the empty plate on top. Staple the left edge of the book. Flip the book and see a mouth-watering sandwich being made before your eyes! (Flip it in reverse, and watch it disappear!)

My Gift Coupon

How can you help someone? Cut out the coupon on the dotted line.
Fill in the coupon. Draw a picture showing what you will do. Color the bow.

To:
_____
_____

Here's a special kind of present.
It's something I can do.
Can you guess who this is for?
It's a gift from me to you!

I promise to: _____
_____
_____
_____

From: _____
_____

ILLUSTRATION: BRUCE VAN PATTER

My Gift to You

Rosie's Gift Goof Up

Rosie decided that the best gifts were things she could make or do herself. Use the clues and logic box to figure out what she gave everyone on her list.

HOW TO FILL IN A LOGIC BOX

When you know that a gift does **NOT** go with a person, put an ✗ in the box.

When you know that a gift **DOES** go with a person, put a ✔ in the box.

THE PEOPLE

Rosie's grandma

Rosie's mom

Rosie's dad

Amy, Rosie's best friend

Jack, Rosie's cousin

THE GIFTS

A poem Rosie wrote

A day of dog sitting

A trip to the grocery store

A painting by Rosie

Ice skating lessons (with Rosie, of course)

THE CLUES

1. Rosie's father and grandma are both very allergic to animal fur.

2. Rosie made her dad's present in art class.

3. Rosie's gift to her mom involves spending time together.

4. Amy's only pet is a goldfish.

5. Rosie's grandma broke her hip last year and has a hard time getting around.

	Grandma	Mom	Dad	Amy	Jack
poem					
dog sitting					
trip to store					
painting					
skating lessons					

READY FOR ANOTHER CHALLENGE? After you've completed the box above, use the clues below to figure out *when* each person received his or her gift! This time, set up your own logic box on the other side of this paper.

1. Rosie started on Saturday and finished on Wednesday. She gave one gift each day and did not skip any days.

2. Rosie's mom got her gift on a weekend.

3. Rosie spent Tuesday dog sitting.

4. Amy was the third person to get a gift.

5. The grocery store is closed on Sundays.

6. Rosie delivered the painting two days before the poem.

Name

ILLUSTRATIONS: BRUCE VAN PATTER

Story Scramble

Read the story and unscramble the missing words.
Write the words on the lines.

Emily and Ryan had a problem. It was the day before their family's holiday dinner, and they still did not have a **IGTF** _____ for their mom. They talked about it on their way home from **LOSOCH** _____ .

"We could give her a hair clip," suggested Emily.

"But her hair is short," said Ryan. "How about a videotape?"

"No. She never watches **ELVIOSENTI** _____ ," replied Emily.

"How about a new sweater?" asked Ryan.

"We don't have enough **MNYOE** _____ for that," sighed Emily. "We'll have to think of something tomorrow."

The next morning, Emily and Ryan woke up early. They were surprised to see that their mom was still in **DBE** _____. "Mom has a bad **OLCD**_____," said Dad. "Will you two help me get everything ready for the big holiday **NIREDN**_____?"

"Sure," said Emily and Ryan, even though they still had to find a gift. The children swept the **LFOROS** _____ and dusted the furniture. They then set the **BLTAE** _____ and helped make the dinner.

Soon the relatives arrived. Mom came down the stairs, sneezing and coughing. She smiled when she saw the clean house and dinner on the table. "Mom," said Ryan, "we wanted to get you a nice present . . ."

"But we ran out of time," said Emily.

"You already **EGAV** _____ me your present," said Mom. "Without your help, we would not be able to have our holiday dinner. You gave a gift of yourselves—the **TSEB** _____ gift I could ever ask for."

Name _____

What Happened First?

These pictures are from the life of Martin Luther King, Jr. Number them in order from 1 to 4. Write the number in the circle.

When Martin grew up, he spoke about his dream that blacks and whites be treated equally.

Martin Luther King, Jr., died in 1968. Today we have a day to remember him.

When Martin was little, black children and white children had to go to different schools.

Martin Luther King, Jr., was born in Georgia in 1929.

Name _____

ILLUSTRATIONS: BRUCE VAN PATTER

My Dream of Equality

CHARACTERS

M.L. (Martin Luther King, Jr.)

ALFRED (Martin Luther King, Jr.'s little brother)

LILIAN (Martin Luther King, Jr.'s friend)

JOHN (Martin Luther King, Jr.'s friend)

MRS. KING (Martin Luther King, Jr.'s mom)

CHORUS

CHORUS: Martin Luther King, Jr., was born in Georgia in 1929. When he was young, his friends often called him M.L. He enjoyed playing tag with his little brother and his pals, both black and white.

ALFRED: I tagged you, M.L. Now it's your turn to be it!

M.L.: OK, ready or not . . . here I come!

JOHN: Wait a minute! I'd better go now. I told my mom I would finish my chores before lunch.

M.L.: I'll come over and help if you want.

JOHN: I don't think that's a good idea, M.L.

M.L.: Why not? The sooner you finish, the sooner we can play!

JOHN: My parents don't want you or Alfred coming by our house. They said it's because we are white and you are black.

LILIAN: My mom and dad said the same thing, M.L.

M.L.: But I don't understand. We're friends, aren't we?

LILIAN: Sure we are. But the rules are the rules. That's why you go to the black school, and we go to the white school.

M.L.: Well, I think the rules are unfair! Black people are just as good as anyone else!

CHORUS: M.L. and Alfred ran home to find their mother. M.L. is upset about what his friends said. Let's see what happens!

MRS. KING: What's the matter, M.L.?

ALFRED: M.L.'s tired of everyone talking about "black" and "white." Skin color is not so important.

MRS. KING: You're right, son. Unfortunately, not everyone understands that.

M.L.: Well, I dream that someday, all people will be treated equally. I will do whatever I can to make my dream come true!

CHORUS: When Martin Luther King, Jr., grew up, he gave many speeches about stopping unfair treatment. He wanted all people to be treated equally. He died in 1968, and today we have a day to remember him.

Walk in M.L.K.'s Shoes!

A board game about events in the life of Martin Luther King, Jr.

START

1929
Martin Luther King, Jr., is born in Atlanta, Georgia.

1930s
King experiences racism and must attend segregated public schools.
Go back one space.

1944
King attends Morehouse College in Georgia.

1948
King decides to become a minister and work for peace and justice.

1963
King delivers his "I Have a Dream" speech to rally support for the Civil Rights Bill.
Move ahead one space.

1964
The Civil Rights Bill becomes law. King wins the Nobel Peace Prize.
You may take another turn.

1953
King marries Coretta Scott.

FINISH
1983
A day is established to remember King.

1968
King is assassinated by James Earl Ray in Memphis, Tennessee, and the nation mourns.
Skip a turn.

1954
King becomes pastor of a Baptist church in Montgomery, Alabama.
Move ahead one space.

1960
King and others are arrested for sitting at a "whites-only" lunch counter.
Skip a turn.

1957
King is president of the Southern Christian Leadership Conference, a group of black leaders.
Move ahead two spaces.

1956
King is arrested for protesting racist policies on city buses. His home is firebombed.
Skip a turn.

Peekaboo!

Cut out the parts. Cut slits on the dotted lines. Slip the tab through the bottom slit from the back, then through the top slit from the front so the clouds show through. Pull the tab to make the groundhog pop up.

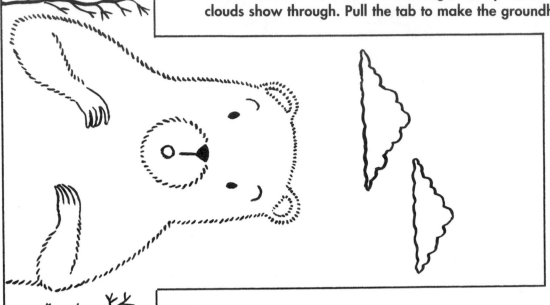

GROUNDHOG LANE

DO NOT KNOCK UNTIL FEB. 2

Happy Chinese New Year!

Each year on a Chinese calendar is named for an animal. There are 12 animals. They are repeated in a cycle every 12 years. Use your animal instincts to answer these questions.

1. 2000 was the Year of the Dragon. Write in the year for each of the other animals on the wheel. Work clockwise around the wheel from the Dragon.

2. What is this year's animal?
   _____

3. In what year were you born?
   _____

   What is the animal?
   _____

4. How old will you be in the next Year of the Dog?
   _____

Name _____

All in a Day's Work

The president is a busy person! Look at the clocks to see when he does each thing. Then answer the questions below.

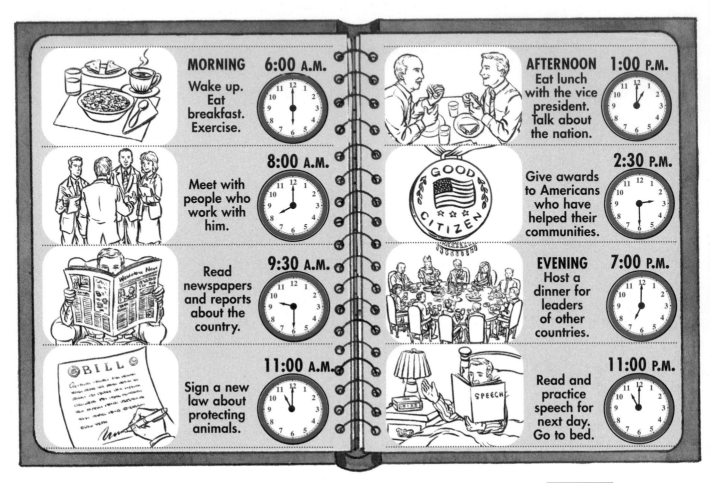

MORNING 6:00 A.M.
Wake up. Eat breakfast. Exercise.

8:00 A.M.
Meet with people who work with him.

9:30 A.M.
Read newspapers and reports about the country.

11:00 A.M.
Sign a new law about protecting animals.

AFTERNOON 1:00 P.M.
Eat lunch with the vice president. Talk about the nation.

2:30 P.M.
Give awards to Americans who have helped their communities.

EVENING 7:00 P.M.
Host a dinner for leaders of other countries.

11:00 P.M.
Read and practice speech for next day. Go to bed.

1. Does the president meet with the people who work with him before or after lunch?_____

2. What does the president do at 11:00 in the morning?_____
_____

3. What time does the president give awards to Americans who have helped their communities? _____

4. What time does the White House dinner start? _____

Name _____

ILLUSTRATIONS: BRUCE VAN PATTER

What Does the President Do?

Research the president's many jobs. Complete the chart by drawing pictures and writing descriptions of some of the things the president does. Then, on the back of this paper, write if you would like to do each of these jobs and explain why or why not.

Name _____

ILLUSTRATION: BRUCE VAN PATTER

If You Were President

One of the president's jobs is to make a budget to show how much of the government's money he wants to spend on different things. After the president creates the budget, Congress must approve it.

Now it's your turn! Follow the directions to tackle your own national budget.

1. Look at the list below. Rewrite the budget items in order of importance to you, with the most important item at the top. You may add an item next to "other" if you think it is important. Then, next to each item, write the percent of the budget you would spend on it. If you do not want to spend money on an item, put 0 percent next to it. Make sure the items add up to 100 percent.

BUDGET ITEMS
✔ **National defense**
   (color *dark blue* on the chart)
✔ **Aid to the needy** (color *orange* on the chart)
✔ **Education** (color *yellow* on the chart)
✔ **Aid to other countries**
   (color *red* on the chart)
✔ **Medical research** (color *pink* on the chart)
✔ **Environment** (color *dark green* on the chart)
✔ **Fighting crime** (color *purple* on the chart)
✔ **Social security for the elderly**
   (color *black* on the chart)
✔ **Health care** (color *light green* on the chart)
✔ **Arts** (color *light blue* on the chart)
✔ **Other:** _____
   (color *gray* on the chart)

2. Now fill in the pie chart showing your budget. Use the colors given in the box above. The chart is divided into ten segments. Each one stands for 10 percent. You can divide one segment in half to make 5 percent, color two segments the same color to make 20 percent, and so on.

ORDER of IMPORTANCE   **PERCENT of the BUDGET**

1. _____   _____
2. _____   _____
3. _____   _____
4. _____   _____
5. _____   _____
6. _____   _____
7. _____   _____
8. _____   _____
9. _____   _____
10. _____   _____
11. _____   _____

_____ **Total: 100%**

Must add up to 100%

Name _____

Women Who Made History

Cut out these trading cards. Read each one and write the answer to the "Find Out More" question on the back. Then, make your own trading cards of other famous women to swap with friends!

SACAGAWEA

1787?-1812?

Job: Explorer

Birthplace: Idaho

Claim to Fame: This Native American guided explorers across the northwestern United States.

Find Out More: Who were the two explorers who traveled with Sacagawea?

SUSAN B. ANTHONY

1820-1906

Job: Women's rights leader

Birthplace: Massachusetts

Claim to Fame: She fought for women's right to vote in state and national elections.

Find Out More: Anthony is known as a great suffragist. What is a suffragist?

HARRIET TUBMAN

1820-1913

Job: Worked to end slavery

Birthplace: Maryland

Claim to Fame: She was born a slave, but fled to freedom and helped hundreds of others escape, too.

Find Out More: Tubman worked on the Underground Railroad. What was it?

AMELIA EARHART

1897-1937?

Job: Pilot

Birthplace: Kansas

Claim to Fame: She was the first woman to fly solo (that means alone) across the Atlantic Ocean.

Find Out More: In what year did Earhart make her famous flight across the Atlantic?

SANDRA DAY O'CONNOR

1930-

Job: Judge

Birthplace: Texas

Claim to Fame: In 1981, she became the first woman judge on the U.S. Supreme Court, our highest court.

Find Out More: How many judges (also called justices) are on the U.S. Supreme Court?

SALLY RIDE

1951-

Job: Astronaut

Birthplace: California

Claim to Fame: In 1983, she became the first American woman to go into space.

Find Out More: What was the name of the space shuttle in which Ride made her historic trip?

Name _____

Women Can Do Anything!

Complete the poem with words from the word box below. The first one is done for you.

Do you know what women can

do ?

They can be doctors and writers,

_____ .

They can fly planes and deliver your

_____ ,

Work a computer, and hammer a

_____ .

Word Box

mail

clowns

too

say

towns

day

nail

Women can be moms and mayors of

_____ ,

Cooks, cab drivers, clerks, and

_____ .

If you're a girl, you'll be a woman one

_____ .

And then you will be happy to

_____ ,

WOMEN CAN DO ANYTHING!

Name _____

ILLUSTRATIONS: BRUCE VAN PATTER

Put Your Stamp on Women's History!

Use the U.S. Postal Service guidelines below to nominate a great American woman to be pictured on a postage stamp. Who knows? Maybe your nominee will appear on a stamp one day!

RULES:

✔ The woman must be American.

✔ The woman must have made an important contribution to history. Women whose contributions are mainly religious will not be considered.

✔ The woman must have died at least ten years ago.

Complete the following information about your nominee:

1. My nomination for a great American woman to appear on a stamp is

_____.

2. She was born on _____ and died on _____.

3. On the back of this sheet of paper, write a paragraph or two about why she is important in American history.

4. What would your stamp look like? Sketch it in the stamp outline.

5. Send this sheet of paper to:
Citizens' Stamp Advisory Committee
c/o Stamp Development
U.S. Postal Service
475 L'Enfant Plaza, SW, Room 4474 #E
Washington, DC 20260-2437

Name _____

Make a Rain Forest

These puzzle pieces show the top, middle, and bottom layers of a rain forest. Cut out the three pieces. Put the puzzle together and paste it onto a piece of construction paper. Then cut out the animals. Paste each animal where it belongs in the forest.

UNDERSTORY

FOREST FLOOR

CANOPY

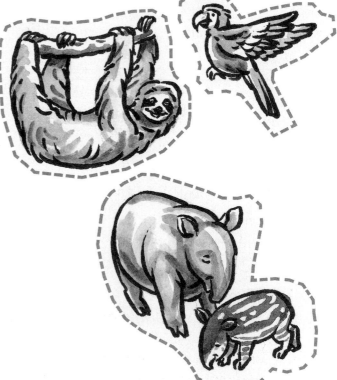

Name _____

All Wet!

How much rain do rain forests get? Look at this pictograph and compare the yearly rainfall for some rain forests and cities in the United States.

Yearly Rainfall

KEY

= 10 inches of rain

= 5 inches of rain

Source: www.worldclimate.com
Note that totals include all forms of precipitation and have been rounded for graphing purposes.

| _____, _____ ____ inches | Las Vegas, Nevada ____ inches | San Francisco, California ____ inches | Chicago, Illinois ____ inches | Atlanta, Georgia ____ inches | Manaus, Brazil ____ inches | Kuala Lumpur, Malaysia ____ inches | Padang, Sumatra ____ inches |

Use the graph to answer the following:

1. What does one raindrop stand for on the graph? _

2. Below the city names on the graph, fill in how much rain each place gets every year.

3. Which place on the graph gets the most rain each year? _

4. How much *more* rain each year does Manaus, Brazil, get than Chicago, Illinois? _ _ _ _ _ _

5. Tropical rain forests receive at least 75 inches of rain each year. Which places on the graph are part of tropical rain forests? _

6. Use an almanac or the Internet to find out how much rain falls in your area or another area of your choice. Add the rainfall amount to the graph.

Name _____

Rain Forest Poster Planner

Tropical rain forests provide a home for millions of creatures. Plus, their plants provide many foods and medicines. But each year, about 50 million acres of rain forest are destroyed. Read about the dangers rain forests face. Then plan a poster to convince people to help save the forests.

SOME RAIN FOREST DANGERS

* Loggers cut down rain-forest trees to make paper and furniture.

* Ranchers turn rain-forest land into grazing land for cows.

* Mining companies pollute rain-forest water.

* Consumers buy furniture made from rain-forest wood and beef from cattle raised on destroyed forest land.

* People take monkeys, parrots, and other animals from the rain forest and sell them as pets.

PLAN YOUR POSTER!

1. Think about what you know about the dangers to rain forests. What message do you want to send to people who read your poster? _____
   _____

2. Write a catchy slogan or title for your poster. It should sum up your message and grab the reader's attention. Keep it short! _____
   _____

3. Write one or two sentences describing the problem. _____
   _____
   _____

4. On the back of this page, sketch a picture that helps get your message across. For example, draw a rain-forest animal threatened by extinction or a problem the forests face.

5. Include a "call to action." That means you tell the reader what he or she can do to help. You might ask the reader to learn more about rain forests, raise money for forests, or take some other action. Be specific! _____
   _____
   _____

USE YOUR PLANNER IDEAS TO CREATE YOUR FINAL VERSION ON POSTERBOARD!

ILLUSTRATIONS: BRUCE VAN PATTER

Name _____

Let's Look at Ladybugs

A ladybug is *symmetrical.* That means it looks the same on both sides.
Draw the rest of the ladybug's body. Then answer the questions.

1. **How many legs does the ladybug have?** _____

2. **How many spots does the ladybug have?** _____

3. **How many eyes does the ladybug have?** _____

4. **What are some of the parts of a ladybug's body?**

   _____

5. **What does a ladybug look like?** _____

   _____

Name _____

Insect Friends and Foes

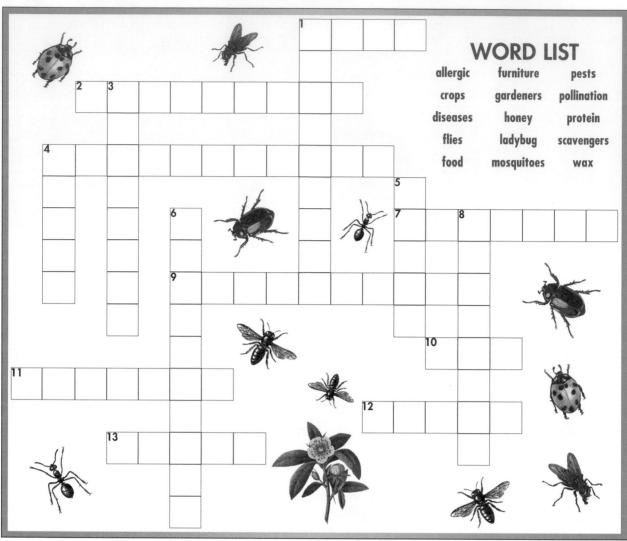

WORD LIST

allergic	furniture	pests
crops	gardeners	pollination
diseases	honey	protein
flies	ladybug	scavengers
food	mosquitoes	wax

Go buggy! Use words from the list above to complete the crossword puzzle.

ACROSS—Insect Friends

1. Insects are an important part of the _____ chain.

2. Some bugs help _____ by eating pests that feed on vegetable plants.

4. Bees carry pollen from flower to flower to help plants grow seeds and fruit. This process is called _____ .

7. A tiny _____ can eat thousands of crop-damaging aphids in one day.

9. Cockroaches are _____ that eat almost anything. Some live in forests and help keep them clean.

10. People make candles from the _____ from bees.

11. In some places in the world, people eat insects as a source of _____ .

12. When bees digest nectar from flowers, they produce sweet _____ .

13. Without bees, we could not grow many fruits, vegetables, and other _____ .

DOWN—Insect Foes

1. Termites weaken buildings and wooden _____ .

3. Wasp and bee stings are a real threat to people who are _____ or especially sensitive to them.

4. Insects that hurt people or property are known as _____ .

5. House _____ can spread germs with their feet.

6. _____ suck blood from people and animals.

8. Some insects spread _____ .

Name _____

94

Detect the Insects!

Insects have six legs and three main body parts (*head, thorax,* and *abdomen*). Most also have two "feelers" that are called *antennae.* (One "feeler" is called an *antenna.*) Look at each picture. Circle YES if the creature is an insect, and NO if it is not. Then unscramble the name of each creepy crawler.

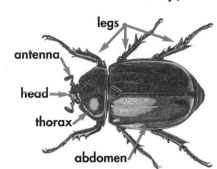

legs
antenna
head
thorax
abdomen

1
Is it an insect?
YES   NO
Unscramble the name: **NOHYE EEB**

_____

2
Is it an insect?
YES   NO
Unscramble the name: **DERIPS**

_____

3
Is it an insect?
YES   NO
Unscramble the name: **TAN**

_____

4
Is it an insect?
YES   NO
Unscramble the name: **GULDAYB**

_____

5
Is it an insect?
YES   NO
Unscramble the name: **MORW**

_____

6
Is it an insect?
YES   NO
Unscramble the name: **MOQTSUIO**

_____

Name _____

ANSWER KEY

PAGE 66
Scoring guide for "What Kind of Friend Are You?" reproducible: For questions 1, 3, 5, and 7, give yourself: 0 points for every A answer, 1 point for every B answer, 2 points for every C answer. For questions 2, 4, and 6, give yourself: 0 points for every A answer, 2 points for every B answer, 1 point for every C answer

PAGE 68

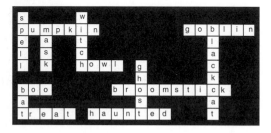

PAGE 70

PAGE 72
1. c, 2. b, 3. d, 4. c

PAGE 73
1. O; 2. O; 3. F; 4. O; 5. F; 6. F;
7. F; 8. O; 9. O; 10. F; 11. O;
12. F; 13. F; 14. O.

PAGE 74
1. 1 teaspoon; 2. water; 3. Put the cornmeal and water in a large pot; 4. 25 minutes.

Page 77
Grandma received the grocery store trip on Wednesday. Mom received the ice skating lessons on Sunday. Dad received the painting on Saturday. Amy received the poem on Monday. Jack received the dog-sitting services on Tuesday.

PAGE 78
gift; school; television; money; bed; cold; dinner; floors; table; gave; best.

PAGE 87
Sacagawea: Meriwether Lewis and William Clark. **Anthony:** one who fights for the right to vote. **Tubman:** a system run by abolitionists who secretly helped southern slaves escape to freedom. **Earhart:** 1932. **O'Connor:** nine judges. **Ride:** space shuttle *Challenger*.

PAGE 88
Do, too; mail, nail; towns, clowns; day, say.

PAGE 91
1. 10 inches; 2. 5 inches, 20 inches, 35 inches, 50 inches, 80 inches, 95 inches,170 inches; 3. Padang, Sumatra; 4. 45 inches; 5. Manaus, Brazil; Kuala Lumpur, Malaysia; Padang, Sumatra; 6. Answers vary.

PAGE 93
1. six; 2. seven; 3. two; 4. (many options): head, eyes, legs; 5. (many options): red, round, small.

PAGE 94

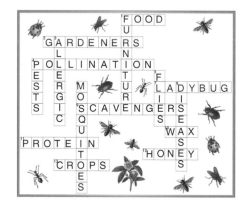

PAGE 95
1. honey bee—yes; 2. spider—no; 3. ant—yes; 4. ladybug—yes; 5. worm—no; 6. mosquito—yes.